SEEKER OF UNITY

By the same author

Helping With Inquiries

Jewish Preaching

'Ask the Rabbi'

Judaism and Theology

Rabbinic Thought in the Talmud

Their Heads in Heaven

Studies in Talmudic Logic and Methodology

SEEKER OF UNITY

The Life and Works of Aaron of Starosselje

by LOUIS JACOBS

Vallentine Mitchell · London

First published in 2006 by Vallentine Mitchell

Catalyst House,	814 N. Franklin Street,
720 Centennial Court,	Chicago, Illinois,
Centennial Park, Elstree WD6 3SY, UK	IL 60610 USA

www.vmbooks.com

Copyright © Louis Jacobs 1966

British Library Cataloguing in Publication Data:
An entry can be found on request

ISBN 978 0 85303 591 6 (Paperback)

Library of Congress Cataloging in Publication Data:
An entry can be found on request

All rights reserved. No part of this publication may be reproduced in any form or by any means, electronic, mechanical, photocopying, reading or otherwise, without the prior permission of Vallentine Mitchell & Co. Ltd.

CONTENTS

PREFACE		9
Chapter		
1	Rabbi Aaron's Life and Works	11
2	The Ten *Sephiroth*	27
3	*Tzimtzum*	49
4	Ḥabad	64
5	Rabbi Aaron's Method	77
6	'En Soph and the Universe	90
7	Man's Worship	113
8	Rabbi Aaron's Scriptural Exegesis	140
9	Summary	152
APPENDIX	*A Letter of Rabbi Yitzhak Isaac Epstein of Homel*	159
Index		165

'*Our master and teacher, the "Middle Rabbi", may his soul rest in Eden, used to say that whenever he recited the words: "Guard the seekers of Thy unity as the apple of Thine eye," he had in mind, in particular, his friend, the holy Rabbi Aaron.*'

H. M. Hielmann: *Beth Rabbi*, Berditchev, 1903, Part I, p. 134

Dedicated to the memory of
BERTHA PREVEZER
בילא רבקה בת ישראל יצחק
beloved sister of Louis J. Mintz

PREFACE

The subject of this study, Rabbi Aaron ben Moses Ha-Levi Horowitz of Starosselje (1766–1828), is a little-known contemplative and Hasidic master, whose thought is of much interest to students of mysticism and religion in general. It has not been possible to avoid the use of the technical terms which abound in his work, but every effort has been made to explain these and keep them to a minimum.

It would have been futile to attempt to understand the thought of an unconventional but orthodox Kabbalist without reference to his Kabbalistic antecedents. To these, Chapters 2, 3 and 4 of the present work are devoted. Chapter 1 is a largely biographical introduction, and Chapter 5 discusses Rabbi Aaron's general approach. Rabbi Aaron's works are three in number: *Sha'are Ha-Yiḥud We-Ha-'Emunah* (his philosophy of religion), *Sha'are 'Abhodah* (his understanding of the meaning of worship) and *'Abhodath Ha-Levi* (his commentaries on the Pentateuch). Chapter 6 deals mainly with the first of these works, Chapter 7 with the second and Chapter 8 with the third. Chapter 9 is an attempted brief summary of Rabbi Aaron's philosophy and a consideration of its significance.

In describing Rabbi Aaron's views it has been necessary to essay the difficult task of extracting, by the use of paraphrase, the kernel of his thought from the intricacies of his Kabbalistic terminology. But, whenever possible, Rabbi Aaron has been allowed to speak for himself through direct quotation from his work in translation. The scheme of transliteration of the Hebrew is the standard one except for words better known in different form, e.g. *Kabbalah* not *Qabbalah*.

CHAPTER ONE

Rabbi Aaron's Life and Works

Students of Jewish mysticism have noted that, with very few exceptions, its exponents and devotees have described the *unio mystica* in such a way that the world and the self still retain their identity and are never absorbed by the divine. However, to some extent in Hasidism in general and in Ḥabad Hasidism in particular, the view finds expression that 'all is in God'.

> *Earth's crammed with heaven,*
> *And every common bush afire with God.*

This view has not infrequently been called pantheistic, but the term is far too imprecise when used for the philosophy of mystics who, because they are Theists, refuse to equate the universe with God as a thorough-going pantheism does. Historically considered, *pantheism* is the doctrine that God is immanent only. He is the universe and the universe is He. *Deism*, on the other hand, holds that God is transcendent only. He is apart from the universe. Conventional *theism* holds that God is both transcendent and immanent. He is other than the universe and yet is in the universe. A new term is required for that mystical philosophy of theism which holds that while God is *more* than the universe, more than a name given to the totality of things, the universe is in Him. There are, in fact, two terms which have been suggested to convey this thought. These are *panentheism*[1] ('all is *in* God') and *acosmism*.[2] These terms, too, are not as precise as one would wish and they require certain qualifications in the absence of a better terminology, but we shall use them in this work for the philosophy to which we have referred. Prominent among Jewish panentheists or acosmists is the subject of this study, Aaron ben Moses Ha-Levi Horowitz.

Unfortunately, we are in possession of very few biographical details regarding Aaron ben Moses.[3] There is hardly any reliable direct information about his character, his physique and bodily health, the impact he had on others during his lifetime, his relationship as a Hasidic master to his followers and the members of other Hasidic groups. The few incontestable facts we do have can be briefly summarized. He was born in the year 1766 in Orsha in the district of Mohilev, and died in Starosselje in the same district on the 30th of September in the year 1828. He was a direct descendant of the famous German Kabbalist, Isaiah Horowitz (*c.* 1555–*c.* 1630), author of *Shene Luḥoth Ha-Berith* (the *Holy Shelah*). Aaron received instruction in both Talmudic learning and the *Kabbalah*, winning recognition for his mastery in these fields. In his youth Aaron became a disciple of Rabbi Schneor Zalman of Liady (1747–1813), the founder of Ḥabad Hasidism. Aaron states that he sat at Schneor Zalman's feet for a period of thirty years and he is, indeed, generally considered to be the favourite and most distinguished pupil of the master. He further claims that his is the authoritative exposition of Schneor Zalman's thought. How far this claim is justified and the extent of Aaron's originality will, it is hoped, become clearer in the course of our study of his ideas.

For a considerable period Aaron and Dobh Baer, Schneor Zalman's son, studied together as devoted friends and companions. Dobh Baer used to say that whenever he recited the words of the mystical prayer: 'Guard the seekers of Thy unity as the apple of Thine eye', he had Aaron in mind in particular. The name is certainly appropriate for a man whose life was dedicated to the theme of God's unity. It was frequently applied to him; the letters forming the verse of the prayer were, for instance, used by the publishers to denote the year in which his books were published. The unity of God is the central theme of all his meditation. The whole of his published work is an attempt to uncover the full implications of the traditional Jewish belief that God is one.

In the course of time a serious quarrel appears to have broken out between Aaron and Dobh Baer.[4] The full details of the controversy are not available, but, apart from the natural rivalry which seems to have developed between son and eventual successor of the master and favourite pupil, there is good warrant for the opinion that the two men differed in their conception of the role of ecstasy in the mystical life. Dobh Baer was exceedingly strict in his rejection of the slightest trace of sham emotion during divine worship; he interpreted in severely intellectual fashion his father's teaching regarding the supreme virtue of the contemplative life. Certainly, profound reflection on the theme of God's unity and uniqueness results in a stirring of heart as well as of mind. Dobh Baer did not attempt to decry religious emotion or mystical ecstasy as such. But he never failed to point out to his followers the psychological and religious objections to the spurious emotions engendered in the process of contemplation. To wallow in emotional religiosity was for him the antithesis of all his father's teaching concerning the need for overcoming the self in divine worship.

Aaron did not disagree with Dobh Baer's contention, but he differed from him both in matters of emphasis and in a more tolerant attitude towards the unauthentic type of ecstasy. While Dobh Baer is said to have recited his prayers in complete stillness and immobility, the reports narrate that Aaron's prayers were of a frightening intensity, an outpouring of religious fervour and enthusiasm expressing itself in a mighty roar as the prayers were pronounced.[5] We shall have occasion to examine the theoretical differences between the two modes of worship in the course of our investigation. For the present it is sufficient to note that the differences were acute enough to compel Aaron to set up a rival Hasidic 'court' in Starosselje after Schneor Zalman's death and Dobh Baer's succession to the leadership of the Ḥabad group. From the year 1813 until his death Aaron's followers were known as Starosseljer Ḥasidim in opposition to Dobh Baer's followers the Lübavitcher Ḥasidim (after the town Lübavitch in which Dobh Baer settled soon after his father's death). Both groups claimed to be the authentic interpreters of Ḥabad theory and practice.

At Dobh Baer's death his son-in-law (and nephew), Menahem Mendel, was proclaimed as his successor in Lübavitch, and report has it that Aaron was pleased that a descendant of the master (Menahem Mendel was a son of Schneor Zalman's daughter) would occupy his throne. Aaron died some ten months after Dobh Baer. Some of his followers then changed their allegiance to Lübavitch; others accepted Aaron's son, Hayyim Raphael, as their master in Starosselje. After a few years, when Hayyim Raphael died without leaving a successor in the Starosselje 'line', some of the diehards among the Starosseljer Ḥasidim preferred to remain without a master rather than be led by a 'stranger'. But the majority of them became followers of Menahem Mendel in Lübavitch or of other Russian masters.[6]

It is impossible to calculate the numerical strength of Aaron's followers during his lifetime. It is certain that they had conventicles of their own in some of the Jewishly inhabited towns of White Russia, since the letters of spiritual guidance and appeals for funds on behalf of the Hasidic settlement in Palestine which Aaron sent to them have been collected and published. However, only two towns are mentioned by name in this correspondence, Slonim and Vitebsk. After the pattern of Hasidic masters, Aaron delivered discourses on Hasidic themes to the *Hasidim* assembled in Starosselje on Sabbaths and festivals. Some of these were written down by his disciples and submitted to him for approval. These, together with autograph notes of the Rabbi, form the bulk of the posthumously published *'Abhodath Ha-Levi* ('The Levite's Worship'). From the title-pages of the two volumes of this work we learn that Aaron had two sons, the above-mentioned Hayyim Raphael and Michael David, as well as a daughter. Her son, Nahman Isaac Jacobson of Shklov, made himself responsible for the publication of the second volume.

After Schneor Zalman, the founder of the movement, Aaron is justly considered as belonging to the five great exponents of *Habad* Hasidism, the others being Schneor Zalman's son, Dobh Baer (1774–1828), and grandson, Menahem Mendel (*c*. 1790–1866), both of Lübavitch, Yitzhak Isaac Ha-Levi Epstein of Homel (1780–1857), and Hillel ben Meir Ha-Levi of Parits (1795–1864). The last two teachers were faithful followers of the first two, unlike Aaron, who, as we have seen, set up a rival 'court' of his own. The inevitable result has been that, for all the respect paid to Aaron's memory in the later *Habad* movement, his writings do not enjoy the same authority as these of the other teachers. Aaron's works are in no way the spiritual fare of the later *Habad Hasidim*.

The objective student of *Habad* thought can recognize that in some ways Aaron's writings are unconventional, and this endows them with a special significance. While many of his ideas are undoubtedly those of Schneor Zalman there is sufficient originality in his thought, if only in the radical conclusions he draws from the doctrine of his master, to justify a separate study of it, though this cannot be undertaken in isolation from the views of Schneor Zalman. In the following pages we shall try to examine in detail Aaron's thought, noting its indebtedness to Schneor Zalman as well as its original elements, and comparing it with the thought of the other *Ḥabad* teachers.

Aaron's main work was published in two complementary parts (actually two volumes of the same work) called respectively *Shaʿare Ha-Yiḥud Wa-'Emunah*[7] ('Gates of Unity and Faith'), Shklov, 1820, and *Shaʿare ʿAbhodah* ('Gates of Divine Worship') Shklov, 1821 (abbreviated here as *SYE* and *SA*). These two massive volumes, running into hundreds of closely printed pages, are each divided into five sections ('Gates') and subdivided into chapters. They form the clearest and most systematic treatment of *panentheism* or *acosmism* in Jewish literature, distinguished by a lucid style, a genius for ordering the extremely difficult material in an almost mathematical progression, profundity of thought, and considerable originality in ideas and presentation. As Aaron observes in his Introductions, the works are to be read as a sustained commentary to Schneor Zalman's classic, *Liqqute 'Amarim* or *Tanya*. The latter was first published in Slavita in 1796 in two parts: (1) *Sepher Shel Benonim* ('Book of the Average Men') dealing with Schneor Zalman's views on human psychology in its relation to the divine; (2) *Shaʿar Ha-Yiḥud We-Ha-'Emunah* ('Gate of Unity and Faith') dealing with the theme of divine unity. In the Shklov edition of 1806 a further part, *'Iggereth Ha-Teshubhah* ('Letter on Repentance'), was added, and a fourth part, *'Iggereth Ha-Qodesh* ('The Holy Letter'), containing selections from Schneor Zalman's letters, was added in a later Shklov edition of 1814. The whole work was subsequently printed many times (the edition used in this investigation is the accurate Vilna edition, 1930) and became known, after its opening word in Hebrew, as the *Tanya*. The little book speedily became a sacred text for the *Ḥabad Ḥasidim*. To this day many of the members of the sect always carry it in the bag containing their prayer shawl.

Aaron planned his work to correspond to Schneor Zalman's book, to which it is a commentary. Thus, the first volume (*SYE*) is an extended commentary to the *second* part of the *Tanya* (bearing virtually the same title), while the bulk of the second volume (*SA*. Gates I–IV inclusive) is a commentary to the *first* part of the *Tanya*. (The reversal of the order is to be explained on the basis of a more logical presentation of the material—the discussion of God's unity logically precedes the discussion of divine worship.) The fifth and final Gate of Aaron's second volume is a commentary to the third part of the *Tanya* and is, in fact, called 'The Door of Repentance' (*Pethaḥ Ha-Teshubhah*). Though Aaron's work is in the nature of a commentary to the *Tanya*, it is not presented as such in a direct fashion, but as an independent discussion of Kabbalistic and Hasidic themes. These two volumes were never reprinted, probably because there was little demand for them by the Ḥabad Ḥasidim, who preferred to study the more 'official' books of the teachers mentioned earlier. However, Gate III of the second volume, subtitled *Shaʿar Ha-Tephillah* ('Gate of Prayer'), was printed separately as a manual of devotion in Miskolc in 1940, together with Aaron's Introduction to the second volume.

Aaron's manuscript notes of his sermons on mystical lore, together with the notes of his disciples, approved by him, were, as stated earlier, published posthumously by his sons and grandsons under the title *ʿAbhodath Ha-Levi*. The first volume, containing sermons on the first three books of the Pentateuch and on the festivals as well as Aaron's letters to his followers,[8] was published by his sons in Lemberg, in 1862. The second volume, published in Warsaw in 1866 by Aaron's grandson, contains sermons on the last two books of the Pentateuch and on the festivals. The title is that of the publishers, not of Aaron himself. The fact that the work consists of disconnected homiletic material is very evident. It has none of the order and system for which the earlier work of Aaron is notable, and there is a good deal of repetition. There are, however, many references to the earlier work and some new light is thrown on Aaron's ideas. (The book is here abbreviated as *AH*.)

A Passover *Haggadah* has been published (*Sod Qedoshim*, Königsberg, 1866, Warsaw, 1866) with Commentaries by Schneor Zalman and Aaron, but a careful examination of this reveals that these are not fresh commentaries at all, but selections on Passover themes from other works of the two teachers. All the comments attributed to Aaron are from his *ʿAbhodath Ha-Levi*.[9]

It is surely not without significance that, in defiance of the established Rabbinic custom of his day, Aaron published his 'Gates' without the approbation of distinguished Rabbis. Did he fear that such approbation would not be forthcoming either because of the unconventionality of his views or because Rabbis might have been reluctant in appearing to favour him against Dobh Baer? Aaron's own explanation is far from convincing: 'Behold, the whole of this work is founded on the holy book of my holy master and teacher, may his soul rest in Eden, known as "The Gate of Unity and Faith", to explain its mysteries and secrets. On the fine gold of his foundations have I built it. Even though there will be found numerous matters and additional ideas not found in his holy book, but these are arranged on the pattern of his holy book and the principles he laid down in it, albeit time prevented him from completing the work in accordance with his holy will and intention. It is for this reason that I have called my work: "The Gates of Unity and Faith", the name of his above-mentioned work.

'Let not the reader be surprised that I have only mentioned his holy book a few times, for I have relied on the Talmudic statement that R. Jacob b. Idi apologised to R. Johanan on behalf of the latter's disciple, R. Eleazar, who gave a decision without mentioning R. Johanan's name: "Everyone knows that whatever R. Eleazar thy disciple expounds is his master's doctrine."[10] I apply this to my humble self. Of all the matters explained in this work there is none which I have not heard and received from his holy mouth. In all our country my constant discipleship with his splendid holiness is known and that I have received doctrine from no other teacher. This is my excuse for failing to turn to the distinguished teachers of the age, the sublime holy ones, to entreat them to issue an approbation to this book.

'Everything found in the book is entirely in accord with his words and holy doctrine. His holy words require no additional support since he was approved and ordained by his holy master, may his soul rest in Eden, and since his greatness, fame and praise are known to many and the earth is full of his praises. Consequently, on this I rely that all the great ones of the generation will certainly grant their approval and offer no objection, God forfend.'[11]

Without doubt Aaron sincerely believed that he was no more than a purveyor of his teacher's thoughts, a mere middleman in the world of the spirit. It must be emphasized that all the Kabbalists believed in transmission from master to disciple as the only legitimate means of acquiring the esoteric divine wisdom. In this very Introduction, Aaron is at pains to point out at length that purely human speculation has no place in Kabbalistic doctrine and that the validity of his teaching on the divine mysteries derives ultimately, like that of all authentic Kabbalists, from the direct knowledge imparted by Elijah, or by means of the Holy Spirit, to the earlier Kabbalists, by whom it was handed down.

Aaron observes:[12] 'All these matters and expositions regarding the knowledge of the root principles have been received by me from the mouth of my holy master and teacher, may his soul rest in Eden, and I have not introduced, God forfend, any new idea on the basis of purely human theorizing. All I have done is to explain them thoroughly, expounding them in a comprehensive manner, that they may be intelligible to all who understand these books, that the basic principles of unity and faith may be grasped with proper discernment and breadth of knowledge. For all the ideas stated in connection with God's unity are based on faith, which is higher than reason. Even though these are very profound intellectual topics, yet for all their intellectual depth the human mind can neither validate nor invalidate them, for they are divine ideas. Just as God Himself does not belong in any way to the category of reason and knowledge, so all which derives from Him in the worlds He has created and His unification with them cannot be assessed at all by means of reason and knowledge, for, with regard to them, all comprehension belongs in the category of the marvellous. But even though they do not belong in the category of of reason, yet they are particularly subtle and profound ideas to the extent that, in relation to divine ideas, all ideas based on human reasoning are as darkness to light and even more so. All these ideas are explained by means of weighty proofs and demonstrations, as the discerning reader will understand if he delves deeply into these expositions, and the gates of light will open unto him.' Thus, Aaron, far from claiming originality, is at pains to deny it. For, to the Kabbalist, original ideas in his own realm, are by definition false ideas. But Aaron does, none the less, refer to his own interpretation of the ideas. He sincerely believed, so far as we can tell, that he was simply recording his master's views, which, in turn, represented the ancient Kabbalistic traditional doctrine. But is it ever possible for a man to be a mere passive agent of another's thoughts, or for him to transmit the thoughts of another without colouring them himself, however slightly? A careful study of Aaron's work demonstrates that, for all his indebtedness to Schneor Zalman, his own system possesses much originality and that, subconsciously, at least, he was sufficiently uneasy as an orthodox Kabbalist to feel obliged to apologize for it at length.

Aaron's second work, '*Abhodath Ha-Levi*, was published with approbations from four Rabbis. These are instructive, too, though not to the same extent as the absence of approbations from the earlier work. The first is from the Rabbi of Lemberg, Joseph Saul Nathanson. As the Rabbi of the town in which the first volume was published, Rabbi Nathanson was naturally approached to give his approval. Rabbi Nathanson did not belong to any Hasidic group and Lemberg was far from the scene of the Ḥabad controversies. His approbation is to be seen, therefore, as no more than a formal response to the request of the publishers. (The same approbation appears, oddly enough, in the second volume published in Warsaw, together with the other three appearing in the Lemberg volume. It is as if the publishers did not bother to collect new approbations and simply printed those they managed to obtain for the first volume. Moreover, the wording in both sets of approbations is almost identical, except for the reference to the sons of the author in the first set, the grandson in the second.) Rabbi Nathanson refers to Aaron's discipleship with Schneor Zalman and to the fact that Aaron added 'many pearls of his own'!

The second approbation is that of Rabbi Yitzhak Isaac of Vitebsk and is dated 25th of Sivan 5602 = 1842. It was thus obtained twenty years before the first volume was actually published! This Rabbi, too, refers to the fact that Aaron's ideas are based on the teachings of Schneor Zalman, but that he added much of his own. A reference is also made to the work published by Aaron himself and that this had won a great reputation for its power to 'inflame hearts seeking God'.

The third approbation is dated 28th of Sivan 5622 = 1862, and is from Menahem Nahum, formerly Rabbi of Polotsk and disciple of Aaron. This Rabbi states that he was shown the work in Shklov when he passed through the town on his way to settle in Palestine. Here there is no reference to Aaron's discipleship with Schneor Zalman, but that he, Menahem Nahum, had sat at Aaron's feet for many years. He testifies that part of the manuscript he had seen was in Aaron's own hand, while the rest was copied by Aaron's disciples, who received the master's approval. The fourth approbation is by Zewi Hirsch, a Rabbinic judge (*dayan*) in Chashniki for over fifty years, and is dated 27th of Tammuz 5622 = 1862.

The approbation of Zewi Hirsch is worth quoting in part: 'It is known among the living the great holy virtue of that saint and holy man, our master and teacher, glorious is the name of his holy teaching, Rabbi Aaron Ha-Levi Horowitz, may his soul rest in Eden and may his merits shield us. Amen. He was a permanent disciple of our holy master, the divine genius, glorious is the name of his holy teaching, Rabbi Schneor Zalman, may his soul rest in Eden and may his merits shield us. Amen. He drew the water of our holy master's teaching and gave it to drink to the flocks which tremble at God's word, which he expounded Sabbath by Sabbath, month by month, and on the festivals. This was his chief purpose, to fix firmly in the heart of each the love and fear of God through the service of the Lord, namely, through prayer.

'Continually did he warn the remnant who longed to hear the words of the living God from him that their efforts and labour in prayer should be with powerful concentration in mind and heart on the meaning of the prayers. He wished them to have in mind the ideas he expounded regarding God's unity and God's attachment to the world in the higher unification and the lower, that in the heavens above and in the earth beneath there is nothing else. He wished that the essence of the idea of self-annihilation, in the category of "nothing else", should remain after prayer for the whole day, even when they were busy in attending to their bodily needs and their worldly occupations.

'It is well-known to all who were near to him how great was his attachment to God, in divine flaming fire, whenever he expounded the word of the Lord regarding the roots and foundations of the unity, as he had received them from his teacher, our holy master. Of him it can be said: "Guard the seekers (*doreshe*, also 'expounders') of Thy unity as the apple of Thine eye".'

Zewi Hirsch states that he knew Aaron all his life, from the days when they were disciples of Rabbi Schneor Zalman. Afterwards, Zewi Hirsch goes on to say, he 'drank with thirst his holy words' when Aaron expounded his ideas both at home and on journeys to his followers.[13] Zewi Hirsch concludes: 'I witnessed his great saintliness, his separation from worldly things, his carefulness in holiness and purity, and all his detailed ways of worship were not hidden from me. He wished to plant in the heart of each the love and fear of God in the ways of *Torah* and worship and God's blessed unity. May his holy merit shield us in the quality of Aaron, lover of Israel, to draw their hearts near to their Father in heaven. In reality, his holy words require the support neither of me nor of my ilk, were it not that the Rabbi's descendants entreated me to have my approbation placed on the frontispiece.'

It is worth nothing that, with the exception of Rabbi Nathanson's formal approbation as the Rabbi of the town in which the first volume was published, the approbations are from Rabbis in the vicinity of Vitebsk (both Polotsk and Chashniki are in the district of Vitebsk), the town in which Aaron's son, Michael David, resided. Two of the three Rabbis were, moreover, Aaron's disciples, while the third was the Rabbi of Vitebsk. One of the approbations was obtained twenty years before the publication of the book, another from a Rabbi passing through Shklov on his way to Palestine, and still another from an agèd minor Rabbinic functionary.

Surely, it is not reading too much into these facts and into the repeated protestations of Aaron's orthodoxy and saintliness that his views were still somewhat suspect as late as 1862. It is certainly highly significant that no approbations appear from the official *Ḥabad* leaders. Menahem Mendel, Dobh Baer's successor as the leader of the sect, was alive and active until the year 1866, and it can hardly be coincidental that his approval is not given to the work, either because it was not sought, or, if sought, was not forthcoming.

The overall impression one gets from the material at our

disposal is of a mystical rebel, inspiring loyalty among his immediate followers and disciples, but viewed with distrust by the more official leaders of *Ḥabad*, partly because of his unconventional ideas, and partly because of his opposition to Lübavitch.

A study of Aaron's views promises, therefore, to be rewarding in revealing a startling, not to say radical, interpretation of *Ḥabad* thought on the idea of God's unity. For the purpose of such a study a considerable amount of background knowledge is essential. Aaron's system is based on the *Kabbalah*, as interpreted by his teacher, Rabbi Schneor Zalman, the founder of *Ḥabad*. It is consequently impossible to begin to understand the system without some knowledge of Kabbalistic ideas, particularly the doctrine, developed in the *Zohar*, of the Ten *Sephiroth*, and the doctrine of Isaac Luria (1534–72) known as *Tzimtzum*. Both of these figure prominently in the work of Schneor Zalman, who, in turn, is indebted to certain earlier Hasidic teachers. Before studying Aaron's views, then, it is necessary to sketch these doctrines. The next three chapters deal with the doctrine of the *Sephiroth*, the *Tzimtzum* doctrine, and the special contribution of *Ḥabad* thought, including the significance of the term *Ḥabad*. The ground will then have been cleared for a more thorough investigation of Aaron's own teachings.

It hardly needs stating that the ideas we shall encounter here will be strange to modern readers. Some of them will seem repellent and have not infrequently been seen as hostile to basic Judaism. But apart from the historical value of an unbiased (it is hoped) investigation of an important period of Jewish thought, the central theme of God's unity cannot fail to be of interest to anyone concerned with religious ideas and speculation.

NOTES TO CHAPTER ONE

[1] The term *panentheism* originated with K. C. F. Krause (1781–1832), V. J. Macquarrie: *Twentieth Century Thought*, SCM Press 1963, p. 274 note 2. Leon Roth uses the term to describe Spinoza's thought, *v. The Legacy of Israel*, Oxford, Clarendon Press, 1927, p. 455. *Cf.* Charles Hartshorne and William L. Reese: *Philosophers Speak of God*, University of Chicago Press, 1953, who use the term not to denote, that 'all is in God' but that God is in some respects infinite and in some finite.

[2] *V.* Gershom G. Scholem: *Major Trends in Jewish Mysticism*, 3rd ed., Thames and Hudson, London, 1955, p. 123: 'An excellent description of the trend towards pure pantheism, or rather acosmism, can be found in a well-known Yiddish novel, F. Schneerson's *Hayim Grawitzer*, and at least one of the famous leaders of Lithuanian Hasidism, Rabbi Aaron Halevi of Starosselje, can be classed among the acosmists. But I do maintain that such tendencies are not characteristic of Jewish mysticism.' The Rev. L. Weiwow has pointed out to me that the term *acosmism* was used by both Solomon Maimon (*Autobiography*, Murray's ed., p. 114) and Hegel (*v.* Benn's *History of Modern Philosophy*, p. 43) to describe Spinoza's system.

[3] *V.* H. M. Hielman: *Beth Rabbi*, Berditchev, 1903, Part I, pp. 133–5; Part II, pp. 6–11 and pp. 19–20; *JE*, Vol. I, p. 16; S. A. Horedezky in *Encyclopedia Judaica*, Vol. I, pp. 82–83; M. Teitelbaum: *Ha-Rabh Mi-Ladi*, Part I, Warsaw, 1910, Part II, Warsaw, 1913, pp. 76 and 86; E. Steinmann: *Sepher Mishnath Ḥabad*, Vol. I, Tel-Aviv, n.d., pp. 387–91; A. Walden: *Shem Ha-Gedolim He-Ḥadash*, Warsaw, 1881, No. 105, p. 18; S. Dubnow: *Toledoth Ha-Ḥasiduth*, Tel-Aviv, 1960, pp. 262 and 391.

[4] *V.* Hielmann, *op. cit.*, Part I, p. 134. Hielmann, who is generally reliable in preserving the family traditions of the *Ḥabad* leaders, states that on Schneor Zalman's return to Liady after his (second) arrest in St. Petersburg, Aaron moved to Liady with his family in order to be near his master, and stayed there for eight years. However, he goes on, a few years before Schneor Zalman's death there was 'much opposition to Aaron'—*qategoria gedolah*—and 'tales were told about him to the master', from which Aaron suffered greatly, Aaron then sold his house in Liady, returning to his home town of Orsha, from which he visited Schneor Zalman from time to time.

'From that time those who had been joined became separated, that is, Aaron and our master (Dobh Baer) and, as is well-known, there were differences between them in matters of divine worship. After Schneor Zalman's death the breach widened, for the men of our fraternity became divided into two groups. One of these urged our master the "Middle Rabbi" (Dobh Baer) to fill his father's place, while the second group urged him (Aaron) to be their master. And so it was. He came to Starosselje, in the district of Mohilev, whence he spread the light of his teaching over the face of the earth by means of the holy method he had mapped out for himself, and they journeyed to him to receive instruction from his holy mouth.'

NOTES

Hielmann's biography enjoys considerable authority among *Ḥabad Ḥasidim* to this day, and it would appear from his rather veiled references that he is being consciously discreet. Hielmann (p. 134 note 3) remarks that once Aaron went to prostrate himself in the mausoleum erected over Schneor Zalman's grave in the town of Gadiyoch, where he was persecuted by the townsfolk who were followers of Dobh Baer. When they refused to give him the key to the mausoleum he climbed in through the window and was unable to climb out again until a smith took pity on him and broke down the door. When Dobh Baer later visited Gadiyoch he rebuked the townsfolk for their behaviour.

There is further interesting material on the controversy in Hielmann, Part II, Chap. 2, pp. 6–11. The use of this source should be approached with caution, as we have noted, particularly since it contains much pious legend, but there is no reason for doubting the basic authenticity of the account it gives of the controversy. Hielmann correctly observes that a careful examination of the works of Dobh Baer and Aaron reveals important differences between them in matters of worship, i.e. Dobh Baer frowns entirely on any sham ecstasy, while Aaron is more tolerant in this matter. Hielmann records that after Schneor Zalman's death Aaron sent letters to a number of *Ḥasidim* suggesting that they come to him to learn the true manner of worship. He further records (p. 7) that many argued in support of Aaron on the grounds that in early Hasidism it was generally the disciple, not the son, who succeeded the master, just as Schneor Zalman had succeeded his master, the *Maggid* of Meseritch and the *Maggid* his master the *Besht*, the founder of the movement.

A disciple of Schneor Zalman is said to have suggested to Dobh Baer that he should leave the district and discover a new field where his ideas would be considered original and fresh! As it is, Dobh Baer, who simply repeats his father's teachings, is unable to satisfy the hunger of the *Ḥasidim* for new ideas. But, eventually, Rabbi Phinehas of Shklov revealed that Schneor Zalman had, in his presence, promised the succession to Dobh Baer. Phinehas sent a letter to this effect to the *Ḥasidim*, which carried much weight.

Hielmann (pp. 9–10) quotes a letter written by Judah Laib, the brother of Schneor Zalman, rebuking Aaron for his ambitions. Judah Laib begins by protesting his friendship for Aaron, but states that he has seen to his dismay the letter Aaron had sent to the *Ḥasidim* from which, reading between the lines, it appears that Aaron is determined to secure compensation for the coolness Dobh Baer had shown to him during the last years of Schneor Zalman. Aaron's excuse that his sole aim is to avoid being persecuted (*nirdaph*) is ingenuous, says Judah Laib.

He recalls that Schneor Zalman had himself mentioned Aaron's complaint of persecution, but the true *Ḥasid* should learn to live with loneliness and rejoice in it, and that Aaron should therefore not feel aggrieved, even though his friends had forsaken him. As a result of his 'persecution complex' Aaron is very unfair to Dobh Baer and is unduly critical of the latter's capacity for leadership. Aaron should be content that everyone considers him to be Schneor Zalman's chief disciple, but they have a higher opinion of Dobh Baer. As for Aaron's complaint that Dobh Baer's manner of worship is 'incomplete and without proper self-sacrifice' this is completely unfounded.

According to Hielmann (p. 10), Aaron was severely critical of Dobh Baer's 'Tract on Ecstasy' (*Qunteros Ha-Hithpaʿaluth*) and concluded a long letter of criticism by stating that he had not yet tackled Dobh Baer's 'Tract on Contemplation' (*Qunteros Ha-Hithbonanuth*), but would find even greater faults when he got around to it. For these two works *v.* the Introduction and bibliography in my translation of the 'Tract on Ecstasy', Vallentine, Mitchell, London, 1963.

⁵ Hielmann, *op. cit.*, Part I, p. 134.

⁶ Hielmann, *op. cit.*, Part I, p. 135. For further details of the controversy between Aaron and Dobh Baer, *v. infra*, pp. 85–86, 115–17, 159f.

⁷ So, incorrectly, on the title-page, but Aaron himself in his Introduction, p. 14a, calls it *Shaʿare Ha-Yiḥud We-Ha-ʾEmunah*.

⁸ These letters are to be found in Part II of the Lemberg volume under the heading of *Liqqutim*. Letters 1 and 2, pp. 1a–5b, are addressed to Aaron's Ḥasidim in general; Letter 3, pp. 5b–6b, to the 'House of Study of the Ḥasidim'; Letter 4, pp. 6b–8a, to the 'House of Study in Slonim'; Letters 5 and 6, pp. 8a–13a, to the Ḥasidim in general; Letter 7, pp. 13b–14b, is an appeal for funds and was sent by Aaron at the request of Schneor Zalman (*v.* Hielmann, *op. cit.*, Part I, p. 134). The Letters on pp. 15b–18b are to the Ḥasidim in Vitebsk, congratulating them on establishing a house of study. From Letter 7 it follows that for a time, at least, Aaron was a trusted 'official' in the 'court' of Schneor Zalman. He appeals for an increase of funds to be sent to Schneor Zalman, because the latter's needs have increased in view of the many Ḥasidim who turn to him for help in the difficult times when it has become hard to earn a living.

It should also be noted that at the end of this section there is a lengthy sermon by Aaron preached on *Rosh Ḥodesh ʾElul* 5562 = 1802. If the date is correct and Hielmann, *op. cit.*, Part I, p. 134, is to be believed that Aaron stayed in Liady for eight years after Schneor Zalman's second arrest and reprieve, this means that the sermon was preached at Liady by Aaron, even though Schneor Zalman was there as master of the group, since Schneor Zalman's second arrest took place in 1800.

⁹ E.g. the introductory comment to the 'Great Sabbath' is really the sermon printed in *AH*, Lev., pp. 1a ff.; the comment on the 'four sons', pp. 14a ff. = *AH, Derushim Le-Pesaḥ*, pp. 2b ff.; the comment on the 'ten plagues', pp. 20a ff. = *AH, Wa-ʾErah*, pp. 16a ff.; the comment on R. Jose, pp. 22a ff. = *AH, Derushim Le-Pesaḥ*, pp. 36 ff.

¹⁰ *V*. Jer. Talmud, *M.Q.* III. 7.

¹¹ *SYE*, Introduction, pp. 14a–b.

NOTES

¹² *SYE*, Introduction, pp. 13a–b.

¹³ Zewi Hirsch also notes that, in addition to Aaron's own manuscript, the work includes the writings of his disciples, which he checked and approved. He remarks that Aaron would certainly have wished these to be published, but he then makes this telling observation. Aaron had been heard to say that the Hasidic works '*Or Ha-Meir* and *Maor ʿEnayim* are not the actual words of their reputed authors, but are their sayings as recorded by their disciples. These disciples 'certainly did not penetrate to the profound depths of their teachers' minds and yet, for all that, they printed the works, and the souls of Israel delight in them and the teachers' lips move in the grave'. *Maor ʿEnayim* is by Menahem Nahum of Tchernobil, printed in Slavita, 1798, '*Or Ha-Meir* by Zeev Wolf of Zhitomer, printed in Koretz, 1798. *V.* the remarks of Dubnow, *op. cit.*, p. 200 and p. 203. Zewi Hirsch also refers to an Introduction printed at the end of the book. No such Introduction is, in fact, printed in either the first or the second volume.

CHAPTER TWO

The Ten Sephiroth

Theism, the belief in an all-good, perfect Being who brought the world into existence, is obliged to face the difficulty not alone of accounting for the existence of evil, but for the existence of anything at all other than God. The world is finite and full of imperfections. It contains diverse objects, and is a prey to contradictions and conflicts. And yet it was created by the One in whom there is neither error nor diversity nor confusion, neither imperfection nor limit. How, then, can the limited and the finite have emerged from the Infinite? This is the central problem of the *Kabbalah*, colouring all Kabbalistic thought.

The reply of the older *Kabbalah*, as represented by the *Zohar*, is that God brought the universe into being through a process of emanation. He caused ten instruments to emanate from Himself, known as the Ten *Sephiroth*.[1] The word *Sephirah* originally meant 'number', although later Kabbalists interpret it as 'brilliance' or 'luminary'.[2] There is much discussion in the Kabbalistic sources on the precise relationship between the *Sephiroth* and God as He is in Himself, known as '*En Soph* ('That Which is Without Limit'). Thus, the problem of the gulf between Creator and His creation is solved by the theory of the *Sephiroth* as the bridge between the two.

The whole doctrine is reminiscent of Gnostic ideas regarding the Demiurge, and indirect Gnostic influence can without doubt be presumed, but the Kabbalists are at great pains to stress the basic unity of '*En Soph* and the *Sephiroth*. In their attempt to avoid the dangers of a dualism completely at variance with traditional Jewish monotheism, the Kabbalists strive to describe this unity with the help of various illustrations. Three of the most popular are: the different-coloured lights in the flame of a glowing coal, which are one with the coal; the different manifestations of the human psyche[3] which, though one, expresses itself in different ways; water poured into coloured bottles, which adopts for the time being the colour of the bottle into which it is poured.[4]

Although the *Zohar* is based on the doctrine of the *Sephiroth*, the conventional names for these, as found in the other Kabbalistic works, are rarely found there—the *Zohar* using terms of its own.[5] It would require a large volume to describe adequately the doctrine in all its ramifications. For our purpose it will suffice to sketch the main ideas, particularly those needed for an understanding of Aaron's system.

It is quite impossible to study the Sephirotic doctrine without coming across such bizarre ideas as a feminine element in the Godhead and a union of the male and female elements expressed in bold sexual imagery. Devotees of the *Kabbalah* have long been embarrassed by these notions (and its opponents have not been slow in seizing on them), which clearly owe much to those ancient pagan mythologies against which the Biblical writers and the Jewish tradition generally fought so vehemently. That we have in the *Kabbalah* a mythology of the divine cannot be denied. Not a few Jewish thinkers have seen this as ample reason for a rejection of the *Kabbalah* as un-Jewish.[6] Others have pointed to the great names among the Kabbalistic authors and have drawn the conclusion that a mythological approach is not, evidently, in itself incompatible with monotheistic belief—provided, of course, that the idea of a plurality of divine beings is totally rejected, something the Kabbalists always try to do. In the writings of Aaron there is a determined effort to 'demythologize' the concepts in order to make them serve the cause of a refined monotheism. By this we do not suggest that Aaron is conscious that he is reinterpreting ancient concepts. A convinced believer in the eternal truth of the *Kabbalah* as divine revelation, he seems to hold sincerely that his view of the meaning of its symbols is that which obtained right from the beginning.

The Sephirotic theory begins by emphasizing the utter incomprehensibility of '*En Soph*, God as He is in Himself. The *via negativa* has quite a respectable history in Jewish thought. Maimonides,[7] for example, holds that only negative attributes can be used of God. Man can only say what God is not, never what He is, since the human mind is incapable of grasping the idea of the divine nature. Positive terms used of God are to be understood as negations of their opposite. When it is said that God is good, the meaning is that He is not evil. When it is said that He is one, the meaning is that there is no plurality in Him. God can be known only through His manifestations. His essence can never be known except to Himself.

The *Kabbalah*, owing much to Neo-Platonism in this matter, is even more radical in its *'En Soph* doctrine. Even negative attributes cannot be applied to *'En Soph*. *'En Soph* is *deus absconditus*. Terms such as 'good' or 'powerful' are applied only to the manifestations of *'En Soph* as *It*[8] becomes revealed to others, i.e. in the Sephirotic realm and beneath it. But *'En Soph Itself* is not referred to even in the Bible, since *It* is beyond all thought and cannot therefore be the subject of human language. It is worth while quoting one or two Zoharic passages dealing with the complete incomprehensibility of *'En Soph*.

Tiqqune Zohar (second Introduction)

'Elijah began his exposition saying: Sovereign of the Universe! Thou art One but not in number (i.e. not like the numeral 'one', after which there is a 'two' and a 'three', or the meaning may be: 'Thou art One but not counted in the number of the *Sephiroth*'). Thou art high above all heights and hidden above all concealment. No thought can grasp Thee at all. Ten perfections hast Thou produced, called the Ten *Sephiroth*, with which to govern both the hidden, unrevealed worlds and the revealed worlds. In them hast Thou hidden Thyself from mankind, but it is Thou that bindest them together in unity.[9] Since Thou art in them, it is accounted to whoever separates one of the ten as if he had caused separation in Thee (i.e. all the *Sephiroth* are united in *'En Soph* and it is forbidden to suggest that any one of them enjoys an independent existence). . . . Sovereign of the Universe! Thou art the Ground of grounds, the Cause of causes who, by means of the spring, waters the tree (i.e. *'En Soph* is the cause of the 'spring', the first of the *Sephiroth*, and this waters the 'tree' of the other, lower *Sephiroth*). That spring is as soul to body, giving life to the body.

'Of Thee there is neither image nor likeness, neither within nor without (i.e. within the Sephirotic realm and outside it). Heaven and earth didst Thou create, bringing forth in them the sun and the moon, the stars and the planets and, on earth, trees and grass and the Garden of Eden, beasts, birds, fishes and humankind, that through them the upper worlds might be known (i.e. God's wisdom is manifest in all creatures), and how the upper worlds are governed and how the upper and lower worlds are discerned. None can know Thee at all. There is no unity in the upper and lower worlds apart from Thee, and Thou art known as Lord of all. Every one of the *Sephiroth* hath a name by which the angels are called but Thou hast no known name. For Thou fillest all names and art the perfection of them all, and when Thou departest from them all the names remain as body without soul. Thou art wise, but not with an intelligible wisdom, Thou art understanding, but not with an intelligible understanding. . . .'

Zohar I, 22b

'R. Simeon began a further exposition, saying: "*See now that I, I am He, and there is no god with Me*" (*Deut. 32:39*). He said: Friends, hear these ancient things which I desire to reveal to you, now that permission from above has been granted for me to utter them. What is it which says: "*See now that I, I am He*"? This is the cause above the highest, that which is called the Cause of causes. It is the Cause of these causes (the *Sephiroth*). For none of these acts at all without obtaining permission from the one above it, as we have explained earlier in connection with: "*Let us make man*" (Gen. 1:26). "Let *us* make" certainly refers to "two", one saying to the one above it: "Let us make" and doing nothing without the permission and command of the one above it (i.e. no *Sephirah* acts on its own but uses the power of the next highest *Sephirah*). And the one above it, too, does nothing without taking counsel of its colleague. But as for the one called "the Cause above all causes" (of which there is none higher and none equal below, as it is said: '*To whom shall ye liken Me, that I should be equal?*' (Is. 40:25)), that one says: "*See now that I, I am He, and there is no god with Me*", from whom I should take counsel, like that of which it is said: "*And God said: Let us make man.*"

'All the company arose saying: Rabbi. Grant us permission to speak at this stage. They said: Did you not explain earlier that the Cause of causes said to *Kether* (the Crown, the first of the *Sephiroth*): "*Let us make man*"? (i.e. the Cause of causes is the term given to the *Sephirah* Ḥokhmah, Wisdom, which has to obtain permission from *Kether*, how then can R. Simeon state that the 'Cause of causes' does not require permission to act?)

'He replied: Let your ears hear what your mouths utter. I said to you that there is one called the "Cause of causes", but that is not the one called: "the Cause *above* all causes". For there is no colleague to the "Cause *above* all causes" with which it should take counsel, for it is unique, before all, and has no partner (*'En Soph* is the 'Cause *above* all causes' and is *above* all the *Sephiroth*). Hence it says: "*See now that I, I am He, and there is no god with Me*", from whom it should take counsel, for it has neither second nor partner nor number. For there is a "one" which represents combination, for instance, male and female, of whom it is said: "For I have called him one" (Is. 51:2) (i.e. the prophet refers to Abraham and Sarah as "one" because male and female *become* one, but there is no compositeness of any kind in *'En Soph*). But this one is without number and partner. Consequently, the verse says: "*And there is no god with Me.*"

'They all rose and prostrated themselves before him, saying: Happy the man whose Master associates with him in revealing mysteries which have not been revealed even to the holy angels.'

Zohar II, 239a

'R. Eleazar asked R. Simeon: The burnt offering is bound up with the holy of holies in order to provide illumination. The attachment of the will of the priest, the Levites and the Israelite ascends (i.e. their intention when the sacrifices is offered ascends on high). How far does it ascend? He replied: We have taught that it ascends to *'En Soph*. For every bond, unity and perfection are hidden in that mystery which cannot be comprehended and known, in which there is the will of all wills. *'En Soph* cannot be known. It does not produce a beginning or an end in the manner in which the primordial *Nothing* produces a beginning and an end (i.e. the first *Sephirah*, *Kether*, produces a 'Beginning' = the *Sephirah*, *Ḥokhmah*, 'Wisdom', and an 'End' = the last *Sephirah*, *Malkhuth*, 'Sovereignty'. Even *Kether* is called *Nothing*, so elevated is it beyond all comprehension. Nothing can be said of it. But *'En Soph* is higher even than this, so that it cannot even be said to produce beginning or end).

'What is meant by "Beginning"? The first point (= *Ḥokhmah*) which is the beginning of all, that which is hidden in thought. And it (=*Kether*) makes the "End" (=*Malkhuth*) which is called: "The end of the matter" (Eccl. 12:13). But there (='*En Soph*) there is *no end* (a pun on '*En Soph*='no end'). There is neither will nor lights nor lamps in that '*En Soph*. All these lamps and lights are dependent upon it, but they cannot reach it (i.e. all the *Sephiroth* depend on '*En Soph*, but even they cannot comprehend it). Only the Supernal Will (=*Kether*), the mystery of of mysteries, the *Nothing*, knows and yet does not know (i.e. only the highest *Sephirah* has some knowledge of '*En Soph* and even this is 'knowledge and yet no knowledge'). When the Supernal Point (=*Hokhmah*) and the World to Come (=*Binah*, 'Understanding', the third *Sephirah*) ascend they know only the scent of it as one smells perfume and catches its scent.'

Zohar I, 15a[10]

'In the beginning, when the will of the king began to take effect, he engraved signs into the divine aura. A dark flame sprang forth from the innermost recess of the mystery of the '*En Soph*, like a fog which forms out of the formless, enclosed in the ring of the aura, neither white nor black, neither red nor green, and of no colour whatever. But when this flame began to assume size and extension, it produced radiant colours. For in the innermost centre of the flame a well sprang forth from which flames poured out upon everything below, hidden in the mysterious secrets of '*En Soph*. The well broke through, and yet did not entirely break through, the ethereal aura which surrounded it. It was entirely unrecognizable until, under the impact of its break-through, a hidden supernal point shone forth. Beyond this point nothing may be known or understood, and therefore it is called *Reshith*, that is "Beginning" (=*Hokhmah*, the second *Sephirah*), the first word of creation.'

In the same vein, one of the greatest of the later Kabbalists, Moses Cordovero (1522–70) writes:[11]

'One must know that it is inadmissible to use the expressions "blessed", "glorified", "praised" and the like of the '*En Soph*, the supreme King of kings, for He cannot be blessed, glorified or praised by others, but it is He who blesses, praises and glorifies, sustaining all from the first point of emanation to the lowest point, from the horned buffalo to the brood of vermin, and before the creation He had no need of emanation, as is well-known. No letter, dot or picture can represent Him when He hides Himself in the recesses of His holy and pure perfection. For no illustration by picture, letter or dot may be postulated of the Crown (*Kether*, the highest *Sephirah*); how much less of the Source of emanation, the supreme King of kings! Of Him nothing may be imagined or postulated or spoken of, neither justice nor mercy, neither wrath nor anger, neither change nor limit, nor process nor any quality whatsoever, neither then before emanation took place nor now after the process of emanation. However, one should know this, that, at first, the *'En Soph* caused to emerge ten ethereal emanations, the *Sephiroth*, in the form of thoughts which were of His essence, united with Him and forming a unity. These *Sephiroth* are the souls of which the ten *Sephiroth* mentioned by name are the garments. These are the instruments of the above-mentioned essence and to these apply justice, mercy and the other attributes which cannot be applied to *'En Soph.* . . .'

Thus, the early Kabbalistic answer to the question of how the finite universe can have emerged from God is, by means of the *Sephiroth*, in which there is to be found the dynamic process of flaw and limitation which eventually causes the divisions in harmony to be observed in the finite world. Of course, this does not really solve the problem, for it can be asked how the process itself can have been set in motion. The *Kabbalah* does not attempt to answer this question, considering it to be a mystery beyond all human understanding. It is for this reason that there is a strong reluctance on the part of the Kabbalists to speak not alone of *'En Soph* but of the first *Sephirah*, *Kether*, the first outgoing impulse, as it were, in *'En Soph*, that by which the whole emanation process is set in motion. We have seen that the Zoharic name for *Kether* is *'Ayin*, 'Nothing'. For of this, too, nothing can be postulated. It is only the second *Sephirah*, *Ḥokhmah*, Wisdom, which functions after the process has received the first impulse, which can be called the 'Beginning'.

What is meant by *Kether*? The word means 'crown'. The figure of a crown on the top of the head is used here not alone to denote that *Kether* is the highest of the *Sephiroth*, but that, unlike the other *Sephiroth*, it does not belong to the body at all but is apart from it. In other words, *Kether* does not really belong to

God's self-revelatory process, but rather provides the bridge between *'En Soph* in repose and Its manifestation in the Sephirotic process. *Kether* represents that which happens in *'En Soph* to cause the completely hidden and mysterious to set out, as it were, on the process of revelation.

It is frequently called 'Will', but this does not mean, as yet, the will to create but the will to will, the emergence of a will in That which is beyond willing. It is as if the Kabbalists, in their reluctance to apply even the ideas of a creative will to *'En Soph* (since will implies limitations—I will to do something I lack), feel obliged to soften the difficulty by interposing the stage of will to will, which, in turn, produces the will to create (=the second *Sephirah*, *Ḥokhmah*, 'Wisdom'). In the words of the Zoharic passage quoted, 'Wisdom' says to *Kether*: 'Let *us* make man.'

The Kabbalists generally frown on reflection, even on *Ḥokhmah* and the third *Sephirah*, *Binah*, 'Understanding', since these have to do with the divine thought processes, but with regard to *Kether* the rejection is far more explicit. To seek to know how the impulse to will can have emerged in That which is beyond will is to seek to know God as He is in Himself. Not only is man utterly incapable of obtaining such knowledge, but it is impious for him to allow his mind to dwell on this mystery. All that is attempted in the Kabbalistic writings is an elevation of *Kether* above all the other *Sephiroth*, while suggesting that in it God's process of self-revelation has begun. This is the probable meaning of the Zoharic passage that, while the other *Sephiroth* have no knowledge at all of *'En Soph*, *Kether* has a knowledge that is no knowledge. But whenever such distinctions are made, there is bound to be a tendency towards dualism. Hence the repeated attempts we have noted to stress that, for all the diversity evident in the process of the divine self-disclosure, *'En Soph* is united with the *Sephiroth*. This passage from the Zohar is typical:

Zohar I, 65a

'Said R. Simeon: I lift up my hand high in prayer. For when the supernal will (=*'En Soph*), high upon high, rests upon the unknown will which can never be grasped (=*Kether*), the concealed head (=*Kether*, i.e. in opposition to *Ḥokhmah*, which is also called "head" but is not so hidden) is most elevated. This head produced that which it produced (i.e. *Kether* produced *Hokhmah*) without becoming known, and illumined that which it illumined, all in concealment. The desire of the supernal thought (=*Hokhmah*) is then to pursue it (=*Kether*) and to be illumined by it (i.e. when the light of '*En Soph* rests on *Kether*, it is the desire of *Hokhmah* to become illumined by *Kether*). A certain curtain becomes stretched (between *Kether* and *Hokhmah*) and, as a result of the pursuit of that supernal thought, there reaches out and yet does not reach out (i.e. at first it is all very faint) through the curtain a light which illumines the curtain to produce whatever illumination it can (i.e. *Hokhmah* becomes faintly illuminated although there is a barrier between it and *Kether*). Then that supernal thought illumines with a concealed, unknown illumination and that thought knows it not. Then the irradiation of that thought which does not know smites against the light of the curtain which stands there and which is illumined from that which is unknown, unknowable and unrevealed.

As a result, the irradiation of the thought which does know smites against the curtain's light, and they both produce illumination. Nine palaces are then formed (i.e. nine *Sephiroth* below *Kether*) in concealment. These palaces are neither lights nor spirits nor souls and none can grasp them (i.e. unlike the actualized *Sephiroth*, which are called 'lights', etc., potential 'palaces' have not yet emerged from their concealment in '*En Soph*). The desire of all these nine lights (figuratively speaking the 'palaces' can also be called 'lights') which exist in thought, which belongs in their number (i.e. *Hokhmah* is one of the nine hidden *Sephiroth*) is to pursue after them (i.e. after thought and *Kether*) as they exist in thought, but they cannot be grasped and are unknown. These grasp neither will nor supernal thought, they comprehend and yet do not comprehend.'

For all the obscurity of this passage, there emerges from it the idea of an unknown, dynamic beginning in which the *Sephiroth* are in a state of potentiality before they become revealed. All this is due to the action of the supernal Crown, *Kether*, the will above willing, the wisdom above wisdom. It should be noted that in this passage the *Sephiroth* are called 'lights'. This name is frequently used of the *Sephiroth* themselves, but in the later

Kabbalah 'lights' is the name given to the irradiation of the light of *'En Soph*. In this scheme the *Sephiroth*, into which the light of *'En Soph* pours, are called 'vessels' or 'bowls'. This is the idea, prominent in the Lurianic *Kabbalah*, of the secret of 'lights' and 'vessels'—*'oroth we-khelim*.

The next stage in the process is the emergence of the two *Sephiroth*, *Hokhmah*, 'Wisdom' and *Binah*, 'Understanding'. These represent the processes of the divine thought in its contemplation of creation. From the will to will there has emerged a will to create. *Hokhmah* represents the details of the creative process as they exist in potentiality in the divine thought. *Binah* represents the details as actualized in the divine thought. On the human analogy, when a man has an idea, not yet worked out in detail, there is *Hokhmah*. When he begins to reflect on the idea and to draw out its implications, to give it substance in his mind, there is *Binah*. *Hokhmah* is the first impulse in God, as it were, to bring that which is not-God into being.

Various symbolic names are given to *Hokhmah* and *Binah*. Thus, *Hokhmah* is called the 'point', *Binah* the 'palace'. The significance of this form of symbolism appears to be that in *Hokhmah* the details are pin-pointed, they have not as yet become actualized even in thought. *Binah*, on the other hand, is the 'palace' in all its length and breadth, in which all the details have emerged from the potential to become actualized in thought. *Hokhmah* is also called *'Abba*, 'Father', *Binah*, *'Imma*, 'Mother'. The meaning is that the active principle, *Hokhmah*, makes an impact on the passive principle, *Binah*, to produce the lower *Sephiroth*, the 'children'. The father's seed grows into a child in the mother's womb.

As we have noted, it is frequently urged that human thought should not dwell on these two *Sephiroth*, which, in reality, are beyond all human comprehension, However, a distinction is drawn between *Hokhmah* and *Binah*. Of *Binah* it is at least possible to ask the question: 'Who?' One can at least ask what it is, although, in the nature of the case, no answer will be forthcoming. One can at least contemplate on the incomprehensible nature of *Binah*. But of *Hokhmah* there can be no contemplation at all. Of it human thought cannot even ask the question: 'Who?'[12]

The word for 'God'—*'Elohim*—in the first verse of Genesis is said to represent the *Sephirah Binah*. Of *Binah* itself there are said to be two aspects. The first, is the 'hidden' *Binah*, of which only the question: 'Who?' (Hebrew, '*Mi*') can be asked, as above. The second, is the aspect of *Binah* as it unfolds to produce the world of created things. This aspect of *Binah* is called 'These' (Hebrew, '*Elleh*). Thus, the *Zohar* interprets mystically, the verse: 'Lift up your eyes on high, And see: who hath created these' (Is. 40:26) not as a question but as a statement of fact. '*Who*' hath created 'These', i.e. *Binah* emerges from its concealed aspect (*Mi*) to its revealed aspect ('*Elleh*). Bolder still, this is said to be the meaning of the Hebrew word for 'God', ''*Elohim*'. The Hebrew letters of this word are those of *Mi* and '*Elleh*. 'God' is a combination of 'Who' and 'These'. This means that of that aspect of Deity beyond *Binah* nothing can be said at all, even questions cannot be asked of It. Even the term 'God' is inappropriate. The God of the Bible and of religion is God at the stage when His hidden nature (represented by 'Who') begins to reveal itself (represented by 'These').[13]

We are now in a position to understand the extremely bold mystical interpretation of the first verse of Genesis.[14] The first word '*Bereshith*', translated in English as 'In the beginning', can be rendered as: '*With* the beginning'. We have seen that the term '*Reshith*', 'Beginning', is the Zoharic name for *Hokhmah*. The order of the Hebrew words '*Be-Reshith Bara 'Elohim*' can mean, not: 'In the beginning God created' but, 'With the "Beginning" He created God' (God being the predicate instead of the subject). The 'He' referred to is '*En Soph*, who is not mentioned directly in the Bible because of this aspect of Deity nothing can be uttered. The meaning is said to be: '*En Soph* by means of the *Sephirah*, *Hokhmah*, created God, the *Sephirah*, *Binah*. Through the divine will to create, the God of religion emerges from its concealment in '*En Soph*.

Thus far we have considered the three highest *Sephiroth*— *Kether*, *Hokhmah* and *Binah*. Because these concern the divine thought, speculation on them is severely discouraged. Cordovero interprets mystically the verse: 'Thou shalt in any wise let the mother go, but the young thou mayest take unto thyself' (Deut. 22:7) to yield the thought that the mind should be restrained from contemplating the 'Mother', i.e. *Binah* and the

Sephiroth above it. The 'young', i.e. lower *Sephiroth*, are legitimate objects of contemplation.[15]

The seven lower *Sephiroth* are divided into two sets of three and the final *Sephirah, Malkhuth,* 'Sovereignty'. *Malkhuth* represents the culmination of the divine will to become revealed. Through it, God's intention to reveal Himself to others, to become 'King' over them, reaches its fulfilment. It is consequently the final aim of the whole Sephirotic process. Hence it is called 'Sovereignty', and all the other *Sephiroth* are said to pour their light into it.

The first triad of lower *Sephiroth* is composed of *Ḥesed*, 'Lovingkindness', *Gebhurah*, 'Power', and *Tiphereth*, 'Beauty'. God's will to create is for the benefit of His creatures. It belongs to the nature of the All-good to share His goodness with others. Thus, *Ḥokhmah*, the divine Wisdom, is said to give birth to *Ḥesed*, the divine Lovingkindness. Now God's lovingkindness is, in reality, a revelation of Himself. But finite creatures cannot endure in the full splendour of the divine light. It is, as it were, impossible for God to give Himself to others, for where there is 'Himself' there cannot be others. The flow of the divine grace must consequently be limited and controlled. This function is performed by *Gebhurah*. God's controlling Power is a manifestation of His love.

The paradox here is that, without the divine restriction of love through the control provided by His power, there can be no love, for there can be no other to love. On the human analogy, the desire to love must have a limited object if it is to find fulfilment. One must love something; one cannot love in the abstract. Since, however, there is divine self-limitation in the emergence of *Gebhurah*, this *Sephirah* is the source of God's judgement. In itself, as it belongs in the rank of the *Sephiroth*, it contains no severity. But, in potentiality, there is at this stage the source of evil, which is caused by a screening of the divine light. To this theme we shall be obliged to return during the course of this exposition.

Ḥesed and *Gebhurah* represent, then, the divine giving of love and withholding of it. For these functions to operate successfully, a harmonizing principle is required. This is provided by the *Sephirah, Tiphereth,* 'Beauty'. True beauty is thought of as a blending in harmony of the severe and the tender. Neither the austere in itself nor the softly sentimental is beautiful. The one repels by its harshness, the other by its sugary sweetness. It is in the harmony of opposites that beauty is achieved. Since the harmonizing principle is at the centre of the whole Sephirotic process, *Tiphereth* is sometimes called the 'body', with *Ḥesed* as the right arm, *Gebhurah* as the left.

By means of the allegorical method, the three *Sephiroth* are symbolically represented by the three Patriarchs. Abraham the magnanimous, sitting at the door of his tent to welcome weary travellers, the friend of God and man, represents *Ḥesed*. Isaac, ready to be sacrificed on the altar, strong in godly fear, represents *Gebhurah*. But neither of these is sufficient in itself. Abraham gives birth to Ishmael, Isaac to Esau. Only the third Patriarch, Jacob, has sons who all follow in his path. Jacob, therefore, represents the harmonizing principle, *Tiphereth*. In his character there is both the *Ḥesed* of Abraham and the *Gebhurah* of Isaac. Jacob is called the man of truth, because truth is to be found neither in unmitigated severity nor in love so limitless as to prevent any actual aim being reached. 'Thou wilt give *truth* to Jacob, *lovingkindness* to Abraham' (Mic. 7:20).

The second trial of *Sephiroth* is composed of: *Netzaḥ*, 'Victory', *Hod*, 'Majesty', and *Yesod*, 'Foundation'. The purpose of God's self-revelation is for Him to reign as King over His creatures. There are two aspects to a king's rule. On the one hand he governs his subjects benevolently. He is concerned for their welfare and takes the necessary steps to make sure they attain it, engaging in war, for instance, when this is necessary. This aspect of the divine rule is represented by *Netzaḥ*. The king must, on the other hand, for all his goodwill towards his subjects, preserve his regal dignity. He must conduct himself with a certain aloofness. His subjects must not be allowed to forget that he is their ruler. This aspect of the divine rule is represented by *Hod*. *Netzaḥ* stems from *Ḥesed*. Benevolent care is the product of lovingkindness. *Hod* stems from *Gebhurah*. Might and power express themselves in domination. It is for this reason that *Netzaḥ* and *Hod* are sometimes referred to as the 'supports' of *Ḥesed* and *Gebhurah*. But *Netzaḥ* and *Hod*, like *Ḥesed* and *Gebhurah*, require their harmonizing principle. This is provided by *Yesod*, 'Foundation'—the foundation and basis of God's desire to reign over His creatures.

Following the method of symbolizing the *Sephiroth* by the Biblical heroes, *Netzaḥ* is represented by Moses, *Hod* by Aaron, and *Yesod* by Joseph. Moses is the faithful shepherd, Aaron the priest who offers sacrifices, and Joseph the righteous man, the *foundation* of the world. Following the analogy of the human body, *Netzaḥ* and *Hod* are the right and left legs, while *Yesod* is the organ of generation. The mythical element in the *Sephirotic* doctrine is seen forcibly in this latter symbol. Opponents of the *Kabbalah* have eagerly seized on this as evidence of pagan notions, reaching back to phallic worship.[16] The Kabbalists themselves retort that these are purely spiritual entities, the source in the upper worlds of what here on earth (after the ideas have assumed an increasingly coarser garb in their descent) becomes human sexuality.

Finally, the *Sephirah Malkhuth*, 'Sovereignty', is the 'sea', into which the other *Sephiroth* pour their light. Through it God's desire to reign over His creatures is prepared in the Sephirotic realm. It is consequently called 'Sovereignty', but, since it receives from all the other *Sephiroth* in order to direct their flow down into the lower worlds, it is described in feminine terms. It is the *Shekhinah*, the divine in-dwelling presence.[17] But in the symbolism of representation by Biblical characters it is represented by *King* David. The *Sephirah Tiphereth*, as the centre of the Sephirotic realm, occupies a particularly important role in the Sephirotic scheme. It is known as 'the Holy One, blessed be He'.

It is basic to the *Kabbalah* that man's deeds have their effect on the upper realms, since he is marvellously fashioned after their pattern. Those spiritual entities in the Sephirotic realm are all mirrored in man. Thus, man's right arm *is* the *Sephirah*, *Ḥesed*, in its lowest manifestation, *Gebhurah* his left arm, *Netzaḥ* his right leg and so on. When man is virtuous, he allows the divine grace to flow freely and establishes, as it were, harmony in the Sephirotic realm. But when he sins, he causes a 'flaw' or 'disharmony' in the Sephirotic realm. God's grace is then prevented from flowing freely, and there is discord on earth.

The idea of man's deeds possessing cosmic significance is the basis of the whole Kabbalistic philosophy. Thus, in a frequently occurring Kabbalistic phrase, man's deeds bring about 'the unification of the Holy One, blessed be He, and His *Shekhinah*'

(=the *Sephirah Tiphereth* with *Malkhuth*) so that there is complete unity above and below. The 'sex mystery' referred to in the *Kabbalah* consists in this that the human sexual act mirrors the 'unification' of the *Sephiroth*. We have already noticed evidence of this kind of symbolism in the relationship between *Hokhmah* and *Binah*, 'Father' and 'Mother'. It is also to be observed in the relationship between the 'active' *Sephiroth* of the right side (*Hokhmah*, *Hesed* and *Netzah*) and the 'passive' Sephiroth of the left (*Binah*, *Gebhurah* and *Hod*). But the main sex symbol of the Kabbalah is in the relationship between the other *Sephiroth* (with *Tiphereth* at the centre) and *Malkhuth*.[18]

The name given to the Sephirotic structure is *'Adam Qadmon*, 'Primordial Man'. This notion can be traced to Philo and the Gnostics.[19] Another term, found particularly in the *Zohar*, is *'Adam 'Ilaya*, 'Supernal Man'. The idea is of man on earth as microcosm. He is the embodiment on earth of those spiritual entities which form the Sephirotic realm, hence the cosmic significance of man's deeds and the use of bodily terms to describe the *Sephiroth*. The *Kabbalah* is not bothered by the problem of anthropomorphism. In this system it is not at all a question of God being described in human terms. Terms like 'leg' and 'arm' really apply to spiritual entities (the influence of the Platonic 'idea' is clear), which only assume human form in the lowest stage of their evolution. It is man who is in the image of God, not God in the image of man. *'Adam Qadmon* or *'Adam 'Ilaya* is the concentration of all the *Sephiroth* emanating from *'En Soph*. Many of the Kabbalists are at pains to point out that although terms like 'first' and 'afterwards' are used in describing the Sephirotic process this should not be taken to mean that the process takes place in Time. These terms are used because humans have no other way of describing a *process*, but, in reality, Time is itself a creation, whereas the Sephirotic realm belongs to the divine thought outside Time.

The Ten *Sephiroth* are now seen to be: (1) *Kether*, 'Crown', (2) *Hokhmah*, 'Wisdom', (3) *Binah*, 'Understanding', (4) *Hesed*, 'Lovingkindness', (5) *Gebhurah*, 'Power', (6) *Tiphereth*, 'Beauty', (7) *Netzah*, 'Victory', (8) *Hod*, 'Majesty', (9) *Yesod*, 'Foundation, (10), *Malkhuth*, 'Sovereignty'.

The following is the diagram used to represent the Sephiroth. *'Adam Qadman* is seen with his back to the observer so that the right-hand *Sephiroth* are the right-hand ones in the diagram:

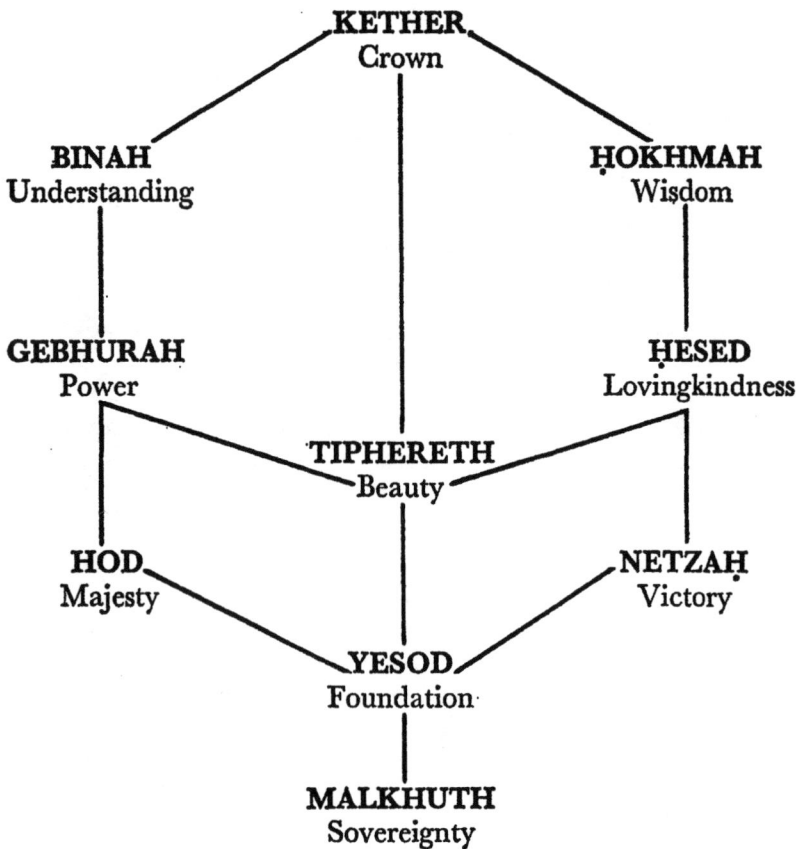

The *Sephiroth* can be grouped together in various ways. One method of classification is the vertical. The *Sephiroth* on the right belong to the 'right line', those on the left to the 'left line', the others to the 'middle line' (=the harmonizing *Sephiroth*). Or they can be grouped in triads, i.e. the first three (belonging to the divine thought and hence beyond all human comprehension), the second and third triad, with *Malkhuth* on its own. In the later *Kabbalah* the six lower *Sephiroth* above *Malkhuth* are grouped together around *Tiphereth*, the central *Sephirah*, so that there is a division into five: (1) *Kether*, (2) *Hokhmah*, (3) *Binah*, (4) *Tiphereth* and the other five, (5) *Malkhuth*. These are represented by the Tetragrammaton. The letters of the Tetra-

THE TEN SEPHIROTH

grammaton are: *Yod, He, Waw, He* (the letter *Waw* has the numerical value of six). *Kether* is too elevated to be represented by any of these letters, but is hinted at in the point of the *Yod*. Thus, we have: (1) Point of *Yod=Kether*, (2) *Yod=Hokhmah*, (3) *He=Binah*, (4) *Waw=Tiphereth* and the other five, (5) *He=Malkhuth*.

Before ending this chapter, it is necessary to refer briefly to the doctrine of the 'Four Worlds', of which there is very little in the *Zohar* (except in the later additions to the work), but which eventually assumed a position of importance in the Kabbalistic system. The world or realm of the *Sephiroth* is known as 'The World of Emanation. (*'Olam Ha-'Atziluth*). The root of the second Hebrew word (*'Atziluth*) is found in Numbers 11:25, describing how the spirit spread from Moses to the elders. The names of the three lower worlds are taken from the verse in Isaiah (43:7): 'Every one that is called by My name, And whom I have *created* for My glory, I have *formed* him, yea, I have *made* him.' The World after the World of Emanation and evolving from it is: 'The World of Creation' (*'Olam Ha-Beriah*). Evolving from this is: 'The World of Formation' (*'Olam Ha-Yetzirah*). Lower still and evolving from this is: 'The World of Action' (*'Olam Ha-'Asiyah*). 'The World of Creation' contains the 'Throne of Glory'. 'The World of Formation' contains the heavenly hosts, the angels. In some Kabbalistic schemes 'The World of Action' is the material cosmos, but in others it is rather the spiritual counterpart and direct source of the material universe.

The whole of being is thus seen as a great chain reaching from *'En Soph* down to the lowest manifestations of the spiritual universe in the material world humans inhabit. World evolves and unfolds from world, all of them infused with what the later Kabbalists call the 'light of *'En Soph*'. The Kabbalists after the *Zohar* to Isaac Luria, and particularly Luria himself, added many elaborations of an extremely complicated nature as well as some entirely new ideas. Those of relevance to Aaron's thought we shall consider in the next chapter.

NOTES TO CHAPTER TWO

[1] *V.* Louis Ginzberg: 'Cabala' in *JE*, Vol. III, pp. 456–79; Gershom G. Scholem: *Major Trends in Jewish Mysticism*, 3rd ed., Thames and Hudson, London, 1955, Sixth Lecture, pp. 205–43; I. Tishbi: *Mishnath Ha-Zohar*, Vol. I, Mosad Bialik, Jerusalem, 1949; A. E. Waite: *The Holy Kabbalah*, Williams and Norgate, London, 1929; M. Teitelbaum: *Ha-Rabh Mi-Ladi*, Warsaw, 1913, Appendix I and II, pp. 233–8; I. S. Ratner: *Le-'Or Ha-Kabbalah*, Abraham Zioni, Tel-Aviv, 1916; S. A. Horodezky: *Torath Ha-Kabbalah Shel Rabbi Moshe Cordovero*, 2nd. ed., Mosad Ha-Rabh Kook, Jerusalem, 1951; and the classical Kabbalistic works cited in the bibliographies in the first three works mentioned in this note.

[2] The earliest reference to the *Ten Sephiroth* is in the mystical work *Sepher Yetzirah*, which probably dates from some time between the third and sixth centuries. Although by *Sephiroth* this work means the ten primordial numbers representing the elements of which the world is composed, the Kabbalists generally read into the work their own conception of the *Sephiroth*. The following passages (*Sepher Yetzirah*, translated with notes by Isidor Kalisch, New York, 1877, pp. 10–12) have been particularly utilized by the later Kabbalists: Chapter I, *Mishnah* 3: '*Ten Sephiroth* out of nothing. Ten and not nine, ten and not eleven. Understand with wisdom and be wise in understanding. Inquire into them, ponder over them, make the matter clear and restore the Creator to His throne.' *Mishnah* 4: '*Ten Sephiroth* out of nothing. They have the following ten infinitudes. The depth of beginning, the depth of end, the depth of good, the depth of evil, the depth of height, the depth of depth, the depth of East, the depth of West, the depth of North, the depth of South. The Lord, the One, God, Faithful King rules over them all from His holy habitation for ever and ever.' *Mishnah* 5: *Ten Sephiroth* out of nothing. Their appearance is like a flash of lightning and they have no end. His word is in them going to and fro. They pursue His speech in longing and bow down before His throne.' *Mishnah* 6: '*Ten Sephiroth* out of nothing. Their end is linked to their beginning, their beginning to their end like a flame attached to a coal. For the Lord is One and there is no second to Him and what wilt thou count before one?' *Mishnah* 7: '*Ten Sephiroth* out of nothing. Keep thy mouth from speaking of them and thy heart from pondering over them. If thy mouth runs to speak and thy heart to ponder return to thy place. For this reason it is said: "And the living creatures ran and returned" (Ezek. 6: 14). The covenant was made for this purpose.' Many of the ideas mentioned here figure prominently, with the new Sephirotic connotation, in the later *Kabbalah*, e.g. that there are only ten *Sephiroth*; that the *Sephiroth* are out of nothing (Hebrew *belimah*, an obscure word); that one must not ponder overmuch the divine mysteries; that there is no counting before 'one', i.e. God is beyond all human comprehension; and the simile of flame and coal to convey the idea of the unification of *'En Soph* and the *Sephiroth*.

NOTES

³ *V.* Joseph Gikatila's *Sha'are 'Orah*, Mantua, 1561, Introduction.

⁴ *V.* Moses Cordovero: *Pardes Rimmonim*, Cracow, 1592, Sha'ar IV, Chapter 4, Horodezky, *op. cit.*, p. 115.

⁵ Except in the later additions to the work, even the name *Sephiroth* is rarely found in the *Zohar*. The common Zoharic expressions for the *Sephiroth* are: *ketharin* ('crowns'), *dargin* ('stages'), *'amudin* ('pillars'), *lebhushin* ('garments'), *setarin* ('sides'), and *'almin* ('worlds'). *V.* Tishbi, *op. cit.*, p. 131. Tishbi's is by far the best and most scholarly treatment of the Zoharic literature and thought. The work should be consulted for the complicated question of the book's authorship and for its excellent exposition of the main Zoharic doctrines.

⁶ *V.* Scholem's (*op. cit.*, pp. 225–39) remarks on this score. Scholem (p. 403 note 75) refers to 'the well documented but very superficial treatise' by S. Rubin: 'Heidenthum und *Kabbala*', Vienna, 1893.

⁷ *Guide for the Perplexed*, I, 58–60.

⁸ *Cf.* Scholem, *op. cit.*, p. 12, who quotes Isaac the Blind's description of the Infinite as 'that which is not conceivable by thinking'. The later Kabbalists, somewhat inconsistently, do, however, use such terms as: *''En Soph*, blessed be He'*, using personal terms. The term *'En Soph* was first used by Azriel of Gerona (1160–1238) in his *Perush 'Eser Sephiroth* in Meir Ibn Gabbai's *Derekh 'Emunah*, Berlin, 1850. Azriel follows the Neo-Platonic view (without, of course, referring to it as such) that nothing can be said at all of God as He is in Himself. Azriel's argument for the *Sephiroth* (p. 2b) is that there is clearly evidence of design in the universe. But the very notion of a Designer implies a lack and the intention to rectify it, but neither of these can be attributed to *'En Soph*, only to the *Sephiroth*. He remarks further (p. 2a): '*That which has no limit is called 'En Soph.*' In reply to the question whether the doctrine of *'En Soph* and the *Sephiroth* is found in Scripture or in the Rabbinic literature, Azriel (p. 4a) replies that since *'En Soph* is beyond all description, there can be no reference to It in sacred literature: 'Know that *'En Soph* cannot be thought of, much less spoken about, even though there is a hint of It in all things, for there is nothing else apart from It. Consequently, It can be contained neither by letter nor name nor writing nor any thing.' *Cf.* article on *'En Soph* in *JE*, Vol. V, pp. 155–6.

The following is the definition of *'En Soph* given by the followers of Luria: 'The supernal light, highest of the high *ad infinitum*, is called *'En Soph*. Its name implies that there are no means of grasping It, either in thought, or in reflection, or in any way at all. It is separate and apart from all thought and precedes all those which have been caused to emanate, created, formed and made. It has no time of beginning or commencement, for It exists always and endures for ever and there is in It no beginning or end whatsoever' (Hayyim Vital: '*Etz Ḥayyim*, Warsaw, 1891, *Sha'ar Ha-Kelalim*, Chap. III. 2.) The Gaon of Vilna (1720–97) goes so far as to say (Com-

NOTES

mentary to *Siphra Di-Tzeniʿutha*, Vilna, 1920, 38a) that one must not think of *'En Soph* at all, not even to affirm Its existence. It is forbidden, strictly speaking, to refer to It at all, not even to call It *'En Soph*. The anonymous author of the work *Maʿarekheth Ha-'Elohuth*, Mantua, 1558, probably contemporaneous with the *Zohar*, remarks (Chap. 7, beg.): 'Know that the *'En Soph* we have mentioned is hinted at neither in the Pentateuch nor the Prophets nor the Hagiographa nor in the Rabbinic literature. But the masters of worship (=the Kabbalists) received a faint hint of It'.

Cordovero, *Pardes, op. cit., Shaʿar* IV, 8, observes that prophet and seer cannot reach even to *Kether*, how much less to *'En Soph*! On the whole question of the 'impersonal' nature of *'En Soph v.* Tishbi, *op. cit.*, p. 100. Tishbi (pp. 101–3) brilliantly analyses the evolution of the *'En Soph* idea. The Sephirotic doctrine owes much to Gnostic ideas of the Demiurge, but, of course, unlike Gnosticism, does not see the *Sephiroth* as separate from the 'hidden God'. The *'En Soph* idea, on the other hand, is Neo-Platonic in origin. If it be asked, continues Tishbi, why the two ideas of the *Sephiroth* (under Gnostic influence) and *'En Soph* (under Neo-Platonic influence) should have come together with the rise of the *Kabbalah* during the twelfth century, the answer is not far to seek. The medieval Jewish philosophers had spoken of God in terms of the Aristotelean philosophy, i.e. in impersonal terms. God was beyond all feeling, emotions and change. This naturally conflicted with the traditional Jewish view of God as Father and Creator. The tension is, indeed, much in evidence in the works of the philosophers themselves. During the twelfth century, therefore, the time was certainly ripe for a viewpoint that would preserve both the concept 'God of the Philosophers' and that of 'God of Abraham, Isaac and Jacob'. Hence, there emerged in the *Kabbalah* the doctrine of two aspects of the Deity—*'En Soph* =God as He is in Himself=the 'God of the Philosophers' and the *Sephiroth*= God in the process of self-revelation=the 'God of Abraham, Isaac and Jacob'. *Cf.* Gershom G. Scholem: *Reshith Ha-Kabbalah* (1150–1250), Schocken, Jerusalem–Tel-Aviv, 1948, and Jacob B. Agus: *Le-Ḥeqer Higgayon Ha-Kabbalah* in *Sepher Ha-Shanah*, ed. M. Ribalow, New York, 1946, pp. 254–79.

[9] The *Zohar* and the majority of the Kabbalists do not look upon the *Sephiroth* as mere intermediaries between God and the universe, but as belonging to the Godhead itself. I.e. in their view God is, as it were, an organism. However, in order to avoid the dangers of plurality, they speak of the *Sephiroth* as manifestations of God as He is revealed, not as He is in Himself=*'En Soph*. In the language of this passage, *'En Soph* is 'hidden' in the *Sephiroth*, but 'binds them together and unites them', *v.* Tishbi, *op. cit.*, pp. 98–99.

[10] Trans. of G. Scholem: *Major Trends, op. cit.*

[11] *'Or Neʿerabh*, Venice, 1587, Section VI.6, p. 25.

[12] *Zohar*, I, 1b.

NOTES

¹³ *Zohar*, I, 1b–2a.

¹⁴ *Zohar*, I, 15a.

¹⁵ *'Or Ne'erabh*, *op. cit.*, Section IV.3, p. 18.

¹⁶ *V*. in particular S. Rubin, *op. cit.*, pp. 119–30.

¹⁷ *Malkhuth* is also called *Keneseth Yisrael*, 'The Community of Israel', i.e. the archetype in the Sephirotic realm of the Community of Israel on earth, since Israel is responsible for revealing God's sovereignty, Hence, when Israel is in exile and there is no harmony on earth, there is discord in the Sephirotic realm and the *Shekhinah* is in exile. The very first passage in the *Zohar* (I, 1a) reads: 'R. Hezekiah began his discourse with the text: "As a lily among the thorns" (Cant. 2:2). What is the lily? It is the Community of Israel. As the lily among the thorns has white and red in it so, too, the Community of Israel has in it both judgement and mercy. Just as the lily has thirteen leaves so, too, the Community of Israel has thirteen qualities of mercy surrounding it on every side. Therefore the word "God" here (i.e. in the first verse of Genesis) is divided by thirteen words from the second reference to "God", representing these thirteen qualities of mercy which protect the Community of Israel. After five words the word "God" is again mentioned. Why is this? To produce five strong leaves which surround the lily. These five are called "salvations" and they are five "gates".' The reference to the Community of Israel is probably to the *Sephirah Malkhuth*. The 'thorns' are the *Qelipoth*, the 'Shells', which surround the good, as the bark the tree or the shell the nut. The word for 'God' in Genesis—*'Elohim*—represents, according to the *Zohar*, the *Sephirah Binah*. From *Binah* flow thirteen qualities of mercy to protect *Malkhuth* from the 'Shells'. The five strong leaves are the five *Sephiroth* above *Malkhuth* (actually six, but *Tiphereth* and *Yesod* are treated as one). Red is the symbol of judgement, white of mercy. Since all the *Sephiroth* flow into *Malkhuth*, it contains both judgement and mercy, *v*. Tishbi, *op. cit.*, p. 235.

¹⁸ It is well known that Rabbi Ezekiel Landau (1713–93), himself a student of the *Kabbalah*, fulminates against the Hasidic practice of reciting before the performance of a religious act the formula: 'To unite the Holy One, blessed be He, with His *Shekhinah*', *v*. his Responsa: *Noda' Bi-Yehudah*, Prague, 1776, No. 197. Another famous Responsum dealing with the *Sephiroth* is that of Rabbi Isaac b. Sheshet (*Ribash*), the great Spanish Talmudist (1326–1408). Here ('*Teshubhath Ribash*', Constantinople. No. 157) there is mention of a certain philosopher who compares the Sephirotic doctrine to the Christian doctrine of the Trinity. The charge of Decatheism was frequently levelled against the *Kabbalah*. This author quotes a Kabbalist who argued that the Kabbalists do not pray to the *Sephiroth*, but when they have in mind the different *Sephiroth* in their prayers, it is to be compared to a request to a king to fulfil his wishes by means of the particular minister responsible for a

NOTES

particular function. The author's own preference is to avoid all this and pray directly to God. On the whole question of intention in prayer as directed to the *Sephiroth v.* the very comprehensive essay of J. G. Weiss in the *Journal of Jewish Studies*, Vol. IX, 1958: 'The *Kavvanoth* of Prayer in Early Hasidism', pp. 163–92.

[19] *V.* Louis Ginzberg's article: 'Adam Ḳadmon' in *JE*, Vol. I, pp. 181–3.

CHAPTER THREE

Tzimtzum

The *Tzimtzum* doctrine receives its full elaboration in t] '*writings of the 'Ari*', which are the Kabbalistic treatises contai ing the theosophic teachings of Rabbi Isaac Luria (1534–72) compiled by Rabbi Hayyim Vital, his pupil. ('*Ari*, 'the Lioı is the name given to Luria after the initial letters of '*Ha-'Elc Rabbi Yitzḥaq*', 'the godly Rabbi Isaac'. His disciples, amoı whom Hayyim Vital was chief, are known as 'the lion cub *Gure Ha-'Ari*.) It is extremely difficult to disentangle the facts Luria's career from the mass of pious legend which has grov around the mysterious and intriguing figure of the great Ka balist, author of a new Kabbalistic system of the widest influen The few incontestable facts can be stated briefly.

Luria was born of German parents (hence he is callɛ *Askenazi*, 'the German'), probably in Jerusalem. Orphaned fro his father at an early age, he was brought up in Cairo by ł mother's brother, Mordecai Francis, a wealthy tax-farmer. I received a good Talmudic education, his main teacher beiı Rabbi Bezalel Ashkenazi, the famous author of the Talmud compendium '*Shittah Mequbbetzeth*'. He was, in addition, student of the *Zohar*, which had been printed not long befo (Mantua, 1558–60; Cremona, 1560). At the age of fifteen] married his cousin, Mordecai Francis's daughter. It is said th for seven years he lived a hermit's life in a little cottage on t] banks of the Nile, in which he meditated on the Kabbalist themes, returning to his home only for the Sabbath. In the yeː 1569, Luria moved to Palestine, where he became the head the famous mystic circle in Safed, the most distinguishɛ member of which was Rabbi Moses Cordovero, the gre theoretician and systematizer of the *Kabbalah*. Luria left veː little in writing, but his expositions of the Kabbalistic mysteri were copied down by Hayyim Vital.[2]

For an understanding of Aaron's thought it is necessary sketch the main refinements and additions, including much th was completely new, which Lurianic *Kabbalah* introduce particularly the *Tzimtzum* doctrine. We shall also have occasion to note the form this doctrine took between the period following Luria's death until the rise of Hasidism, as well as the ideas on the subject by the early Hasidic leaders before the rise of the Ḥabad movement to which Aaron belonged.

We have seen that the Zoharic answer to the problem of how the finite universe emerged from the Infinite is that God caused the *Ten Sephiroth* to emanate from Him. Lurianic *Kabbalah* gives a very different answer. This is that God 'withdrew from Himself into Himself' to leave room for the finite universe. *Tzimtzum* (='withdrawal') is, then, the doctrine according to which God concentrates his being into Himself in order to leave an empty primordial 'space' into which Time and Space as we know them eventually emerged. It must not be thought that Luria (who, in any event, drew on his predecessors) considered his doctrine to be a real innovation. He appears to have believed that his was an authentic exposition of the older *Kabbalah*. Consequently, the Zoharic doctrine of emanation and the *Sephiroth*, far from being abandoned by him, are used as the basis of his system. The idea of divine emanation and divine withdrawal, basically contradictory though they are, become harmonized in the Lurianic system. This is achieved by postulating two stages in the process of God's self-revelation, first withdrawal and then emanation. The first step in the process was God's withdrawal, as a result of which the empty 'space' was created. When God's light later re-entered this 'space', as it had to do for the purpose of creation, it did so in the form of the *Ten Sephiroth*. The process as a whole is now seen as one of both withdrawal and emanation, of God withdrawing Himself in order to allow finite creatures to exist and then sending His divine light in weaker form to sustain them.

The following are the main stages in the divine process of creation as seen by Luria. It will be seen that, although Zoharic symbolism is used, there are, in the new system, many refinements as well as complicated new ideas. It should also be noted that for the Lurianic Kabbalists these stages do not take place in Time at all, although terms suggesting a time sequence are used inevitably, but belong to the eternal process taking place outside Time altogether.

There can be no doubt from the facts we have that Luria was

TZIMTZUM

a personality dedicated to the pursuit of holiness and devoted to a life of severe contemplation. Bizarre and repellent though some of the details of his system seem, it is certain that for him they were interpreted in a purely spiritual way and are the products of years of mystic meditation. The majority of the Kabbalists accept the Lurianic *Kabbalah* as a divine revelation on a par with that of the *Zohar*. These secrets were believed to have been revealed to him by Elijah. However, a student of the *Kabbalah* like the Vilna Gaon, who accepted the *Zohar* as revealed truth, looked upon Luria's system as an extremely brilliant but purely human composition, with which it was permissible to disagree.[3] For our purpose it is sufficient to note that Hasidism in general and *Ḥabad* in particular accept the Lurianic *Kabbalah* as a revelation of divine truth.

We have seen that, for the earlier *Kabbalah*, the first stage in the whole process of divine self-revelation is the emergence of *Kether*, the divine 'Will', from potentiality to actuality, in *'En Soph*. Lurianic *Kabbalah*, on the other hand, begins with the idea of *Tzimtzum*. *'En Soph* withdraws into Itself, leaving a primordial 'Space' (*Ḥalal*). Into this 'Empty Space' a 'line' (*qaw*) of the divine light is propelled, for without it nothing could have existed. (Although the 'Space' was left empty of *'En Soph*, a faint 'residue'—*Reshimu*—of the divine light remained. In some of the writings of the post-Lurianic Kabbalists very little mention of this 'residue' is made; in others it is referred to frequently.) Since the *Sephirah Malkhuth*, 'Sovereignty', is, in the older *Kabbalah*, the name for the final manifestation of *'En Soph* in the Sephirotic realm, the Lurianic *Kabbalah* calls the 'Empty Space', '*Malkhuth Di-'En Soph*', 'The Sovereignty of *'En Soph*', i.e. the last vestiges, as it were, of *'En Soph* before the process of God's self-enfolding begins.

The 'line' of *'En Soph*'s light, as it pervades the 'Empty Space', produces *'Adam Qadmon*, 'Primordial Man'. We have already come across this term in our examination of the Zoharic teaching, but the meaning is not quite the same in the Lurianic Kabbalah. In the earlier *Kabbalah 'Adam Qadmon* is the name given to the totality of the *Sephiroth*. In the Lurianic *Kabbalah*, on the other hand, *'Adam Qadmon* is a kind of intermediary between *'En Soph* and the *Sephiroth*. The *Sephiroth* are contained in potentiality in *'Adam Qadmon*. They do not emerge into actuality until the stage known as '*Olam Ha-'Atziluth*, 'The World of Emanation'. But since the Sephirotic symbolism is used of all the stages of the process (we have seen that the term *Malkhuth* is used even of the '*En Soph* stage) the final stage of '*Adam Qadmon* is called: '*Malkhuth Di-'Adam Qadmon* ('Sovereignty of '*Adam Qadmon*'). This final stage becomes the first stage in 'The World of Emanation' and is therefore also called: '*Kether*' of 'The World of Emanation' (just as *Malkhuth* of '*En Soph* is, at the same time, *Kether* of '*Adam Qadmon*). In like manner *Malkhuth* of this world becomes *Kether* of the next lowest world ('The World of Creation') and, in turn, *Malkhuth* of this becomes *Kether* of 'The World of Formation' and *Malkhuth* of this *Kether* of 'The World of Action'.

To revert to the beginning of the process, the light of '*En Soph* which emerged into the 'Empty Space' to produce '*Adam Qadmon*, produces, in turn, the *Ten Sephiroth*. These are known as the 'vessels' (*kelim*) in that they contain the 'lights' ('*oroth*) of '*En Soph*. There then occurred the catastrophic event which Lurianic *Kabbalah* calls 'the breaking of the vessels'. Another name for this is, following a passage in the *Zohar*, 'the death of the kings', after the verses describing the kings who ruled in Edom 'before there reigned any king over the children of Israel' (Gen. 36:31–39). What is meant by these mysterious allusions? The light of '*En Soph*, returning to the 'Empty Space', was, at first, too powerful to be contained by the seven lower *Sephiroth* (*Ḥesed* to *Malkhuth*), with the result that these were shattered by its impact.

In this way the Lurianic *Kabbalah* seeks to explain the ultimate origin of evil and imperfection as a kind of cosmic flaw reaching back to the divine creative process itself. The theory behind it appears to be that God Himself cannot bring the finite world into being without travail, because tension is bound to result from the emergence of the finite out of the Infinite. The 'breaking of the vessels' set in motion a process by which sparks of holiness became scattered in all things. It is the task of man, in pursuing the good and avoiding evil, to reclaim these 'sparks' for the holy and thus heal the primordial breach. The task of reclamation is known as '*Tiqqun*' ('putting right', 'perfecting'). When the work of '*Tiqqun*' is complete, the Messiah will come and complete harmony will be restored to creation.

The *Shekhinah* will be brought back from exile (it must be realized that in the *Kabbalah* the 'exile of the *Shekhinah*' means that a part of God is, as it were, exiled from God) and God's kingdom established. Every good deed of man brings the process nearer to its culmination. Every evil deed produces a 'flaw' (*pegam*) which arrests the process. Through man's deeds, God is building Jerusalem every day.

This highly charged mythical doctrine of *tiqqun* and *pegam*, of 'putting right' and producing 'flaws', and of reclaiming the 'holy sparks' in order to bring the Messiah, became the most powerful stimulus to Jewish Messianism. In the heretical mystical movement founded by the false Messiah, Shabbethai Zewi (1626–76), the doctrine was allowed to embrace the notion that sin may, on occasion, be engaged in freely for the purpose of reclaiming those 'sparks' that had fallen into the domain of the evil. It is no accident that some of Shabbethai Zewi's followers continued to believe in him as the Messiah even after he had embraced the Muslim faith! It was because of aberrations of this kind that the Lurianic *Kabbalah* later fell into disfavour or, at least, attempts were made to restrict the study of *Kabbalah* to sages of mature years.

After the 'breaking of the vessels' or the 'death of the kings' the *Sephiroth* were re-formed. However, the new 'vessels' were no longer 'simple' *Sephiroth*, but *Sephiroth* in combinations of various kinds, so that they could, as it were, aid one another. These combinations are known as '*Partzuphim*' ('Figures' or 'Faces'). Since man has a cosmic role to play, according to the *Kabbalah*, he is in a position to control, by his deeds, the formation of these 'Figures'. The true adept, familiar with all the various combinations, is able to have the intention of bringing the combinations about when he carries out the precepts of Judaism. No detail in the performance of the precepts is devoid of meaning, for each is required to produce a particular cosmic effect. Much of the Lurianic *Kabbalah* is taken up with the complicated combinations which form the '*Partzuphim*'. But the five chief '*Partzuphim*' are: (1) '*Arikh 'Anpin* (lit. 'Long Face', but meaning 'Long Suffering'), equivalent to the *Sephirah Kether*; (2) '*Abba* ('Father', equivalent to the *Sephirah Ḥokhmah*; (3) '*Imma* ('Mother', equivalent to the *Sephirah Binah*); (4) *Zeʿer 'Anpin* (lit. 'Little Face', but meaning the opposite of 'slow to anger' = '*Arikh 'Anpin*), the equivalent of the six *Sephiroth* grouped around *Tiphereth* (*Ḥesed* to *Yesod*); (5) *Nuqwah* (the 'Female', equivalent to the *Sephirah Malkhuth*).

In the earlier system the unification of 'the Holy One, blessed be He' and His *Shekhinah* means, as we have seen, the unification of the *Sephiroth* of *Tiphereth* and *Malkhuth*. In the Lurianic *Kabbalah* the unification is that of *Zeʿer 'Anpin* (generally called simply *Zeʿer*) and *Nuqwah*, e.g. the six *Sephiroth* grouped around *Tiphereth* with *Malkhuth*. The whole point of the *Partzuphim* idea appears to be that while the *Sephiroth* in isolation, as it were, cannot endure the light of *'En Soph* they can, in combination, help each other to endure that light. That is to say, the unfolding of the Infinite to produce the finite can only be effective if the mediating instruments attain to an existence in which they are part of a single organism. The *Partzuphim* are a kind of re-organization of the *Sephiroth*, after the 'breaking of the vessels', for the purpose of *Tiqqun*.

Why were the 'vessels' broken? Why could God not have produced the *Sephiroth* in their 'unbreakable' form? The answer is far from clearly stated, but something like the following idea, to which we have already called attention, seems to be implied. Whatever purpose evil plays in God's creation, it must also have its source in God. But, in the early stages of God's self-unfolding, evil is only latent, as it were, in God's complete justice and mercy. It is only in the process of creation that evil comes to enjoy an independent existence. The origin of evil goes back ultimately to the *Tzimtzum* process, for that is precisely what evil is, the absence of God. Thus, in the very process of *Tzimtzum*, which, as God's self-disclosure, is for the benefit of creatures, the germs of evil are contained. Without God there is bound to be evil, but, and here lies the paradox, there can only be finite creatures if there is that absence of God represented by *Tzimtzum*. Through the 'breaking of the vessels' the evil begins to be separated from the good. Eventually, the process results in the emergence of the denizens of the 'Other Side' (*Sitra 'Aḥara*), the demonic side of existence, and the *Qelipoth*, the 'Shells', which surround the good as the bark the tree, the husk the kernel. The realm of the *Sephiroth* after the 'breaking of the vessels' and their re-emergence as the *Partzuphim* is now the 'World of *Tiqqun*'. The fight of the good against the evil has now begun, in potentiality at least, and room is left for man's cosmic task of completing the *Tiqqun*, the work of perfecting and rectifying.

To explore further the subtleties of the Lurianic *Kabbalah* and its bewildering elaborations is beyond the scope of our inquiry. We have, however, to examine how the *Tzimtzum* doctrine fared among the post-Lurianic Kabbalists.[4]

Teitelbaum concludes, from the numerous warnings by the disciples of Luria against receiving ideas like *Tzimtzum*, the 'line' and the 'empty space' in anything but a metaphorical manner, that there were not a few to be found who interpreted the whole system in a grossly material way. The Italian Rabbi and Kabbalist, Joseph Ergas (1685–1730), in his famous dialogue between a philosopher and a Kabbalist writes:[5] 'Whoever wishes to understand the notion of *Tzimtzum* literally falls into numerous errors and denials of the main principles of faith ... For '*En Soph* has neither image nor form such as the form of a surrounding circle with an empty space in the middle, into which a line of light emerges, for if this were so He would have an image, God forfend ... Apart from this it is said that there is no place from which He is absent, above without end, below without limit, and in every direction. But if *Tzimtzum* is taken literally then there is a place from which He *is* absent, since all that emerges into the empty space is a line as thin as a thread ... Similarly, all the Kabbalists agree that '*En Soph* is always in the state of unchanging being and no events, not even the events of the soul, can affect Him in any way. Perforce one is obliged to conclude that the *Tzimtzum* doctrine is not to be taken literally. The clear truth in the matter is that this is in the nature of a parable, an aid to comprehension.'

Among others, Immanuel Hay Ricchi (1688–1743), another Italian Kabbalist, attacked Joseph Ergas's view, insisting that the *Tzimtzum* doctrine has to be understood literally. His argument runs that, since the whole purpose of the *Tzimtzum* idea is to explain the emergence of the finite world from the Infinite, the purpose is defeated unless the doctrine means what it says. If Ergas is right and the doctrine is only a parable, it must follow that there has been no real withdrawal and God is, therefore, present in material things, even in the unworthy and the evil. Rather than accept such a conclusion, Ricchi is prepared to interpret the doctrine to mean that God really did withdraw Himself and it is only His providence, not His true being, which extends to the 'Empty Space'. To say that the king gazes through his windows at filth is one thing. To say that he is immersed in filth is quite another. Ricchi maintains that Ergas has completely misunderstood Luria and that his, Ricchi's, is the only authentic interpretation of the master's teaching.[6]

Dobh Baer, *Maggid* of Meseritch (1710–72), leader of the Hasidic movement after the death of its founder, the *Ba'al Shem Tobh*, builds on the ideas of the founder of the movement as well as upon other Kabbalistic predecessors in describing the *Tzimtzum* doctrine. To illustrate the doctrine, Dobh Baer uses the parable of a father in relation to his small son. In order to converse with his child, the father forsakes his adult interests to engage in baby talk. Similarly, God 'lowers' Himself in the act of *Tzimtzum* in order to have creatures with whom He can converse.[7] Another illustration in similar vein is that of the father who, seeing his little boy playing in the street, pretends not to notice him, so that the boy will run after the father and thereby demonstrate that his father's love means more to him than his games. God performs the act of *Tzimtzum*, causing Him to become 'hidden'. As a result man, too, performs an act of *Tzimtzum*, withdrawing from worldly matters to run after God.[8]

Of particular importance, as containing an idea later to be developed fully in *Ḥabad*, is Dobh Baer's illustration of the 'shield' which screens the sun's light. Just as the 'shield' has the effect of reducing the sun's light in order that creatures might benefit from the sun without being harmed by it, so God brings about the *Tzimtzum* in order that His creatures might endure to enjoy the light of His presence.[9] This is said to be the mystical interpretation of: 'For the Lord God is a sun and a shield' (Ps. 84:12). The term 'Lord' (= the Tetragrammaton) is the name for God in His aspect of mercy, as the Rabbis say. The term 'God', on the other hand, refers to His aspect of judgement. God's withdrawal is His judgement, it is the control of His divine mercy. And yet since this very withdrawal is for the benefit of creatures that they might endure, His judgement is itself mercy. God is, therefore, both a 'sun' and a 'shield'. The *Tzimtzum* provides the screen or 'shield' for the purpose of mediating the divine light, without which no creatures could exist, but which requires to be 'screened' if they are to exist.[10] Thus, for Dobh Baer, *Tzimtzum* is really a screening of the divine light, rather than an actual withdrawal of God. Ḥabad thought is firmly based on this idea, which it develops and upon which it offers various elaborations.

It is difficult to know what the views on *Tzimtzum* were of the founder of the Hasidic movement, since he left none in writing. In this, as in other matters, one must rely, with some degree of caution, on the writings of his disciples, when they speak in his name. A famous collection of the sayings of the *Besht*, the founder of Hasidism, was made by Aaron ben Zewi of Opatow and published under the title: '*Kether Shem Tobh*' ('The Crown of Shem Tobh' = 'The Good Name', Zolkiew, 1794–5). It appears that, in drawing on the *Tzimtzum* idea, the *Besht* laid special emphasis on its psychological meaning, on its significance for the soul-life of man. In this, as in other matters, early Hasidism is less interested in the *Kabbalah* as a theosophical system than in its implications for man's inner life. Thus, the whole *Tzimtzum* process is said to be mirrored in man's psyche. By delving deeply into his own nature, man can come to know God. The *Besht* is reported as teaching that the whole Sephirotic process takes place in man's soul whenever he discovers some new idea in the *Torah*. The *Sephiroth* of Ḥokhmah and *Binah* are the sources of the new idea. This intuitive notion is, at first, boundless, i.e. its full meaning has not yet been pinned down, hence at this stage there is also a correspondence with the *Sephirah* of Ḥesed, boundless and unlimited in its love.

When the idea is finally pinned down by the mind, when it is limited and thus saved from vagueness, a process operates in the mind similar to that of *Gebhurah* in the Sephirotic realm. In this way the *Tzimtzum* process is repeated in man's creative thinking. By controlling his thoughts and arranging them in ordered sequence so that they can be communicated to others, he repeats the *Tzimtzum* process and mirrors it. The harmony between the idea in its unlimited stage and the idea in severe control is effected by the *Sephirah* of *Tiphereth*, the harmonizing principle. Then, the thinker must have faith in his idea as well as faith in the *Torah* it is intended to elucidate, and this faith corresponds to the *supporting Sephiroth* of *Netzaḥ* and *Hod*. There follows delight in the idea, which corresponds to *Yesod*, representing the 'organ of pleasure'. Finally, the idea is conveyed in speech, and this final revelation corresponds to the last of the *Sephiroth*, *Malkhuth*, the *Sephirah* which reveals the whole process. God, too, the exposition concludes, created the 'upper worlds' by 'studying' the 'secrets of the *Torah*' and then the 'revealed worlds' by 'studying' the 'revealed *Torah*'.[11]

The well-known parable of the *Besht* is highly relevant to the form *Tzimtzum* assumes in Ḥabad thought. A mighty king sat on his throne, situated in the centre of a huge palace with many halls, all of them filled with gold and silver and precious stones. Those servants of the king who were far more interested in acquiring wealth than in gazing at the king's splendour spent all their time, when they were admitted to the palace, in the outer halls, gathering the treasures they found there. So engrossed were they in this that they never saw the countenance of the king. But the wise servants, refusing to be distracted by the treasures in the halls, pressed on until they came to the king on his throne in the centre of the palace. To their astonishment, once they reached the king's presence, they discovered that the palace, its halls and their treasures were really only an illusion, created by the king's magic powers. In the same way, God hides Himself in the 'garments' and 'barriers' of the upper worlds and the cosmos. When man recognizes that this is so, when he acknowledges that all is created out of God's essence—'like the snail whose shell is formed of itself'—and that, in reality, there are no barriers between man and his God, all 'the workers of iniquity' are dispersed. This parable, in its context, refers to prayer. Man should persist in his devotions and refuse to be distracted by extraneous thoughts. But the idea that all is in God is clearly implied. The 'snail' illustration is frequently quoted in Ḥabad literature.[12]

A further saying attributed to the *Besht* is on the meaning of the love of God: 'And thou shalt love the Lord thy God' (*Deut.* 6:5). The Lord (=the Tetragrammaton) is the divine name representing God's mercy. 'Thy God' ('*Elohim*) is the divine name representing God's judgement. This latter is the ultimate source of evil and suffering but these are the inevitable results of *Tzimtzum*, the withdrawal of God. However, unless *Tzimtzum* had taken place, there would have been neither world nor creatures. Hence, the very judgement of God is, in reality, His mercy. When man accepts his sufferings in love as coming from God, he acknowledges that 'the Lord' is 'God', i.e. that all is, in reality, mercy. In the process of loving God man acknowledges that God is all-good.[13]

Some further ideas on *Tzimtzum* from the *Besht* or his school are found in the early Hasidic work: '*Tzawaath Ha-Ribhash*' ('The Will of Israel the Ba'al Shem').[14] Here in particular the psychological implications of the *Tzimtzum* doctrine are drawn. In a homily on 'attachment' to God—*debhequth*—it is said that all 'worlds' are as nothing to God, since they appear in the 'Empty Space' vacated by Him through *Tzimtzum*, the whole process being effected merely by a single divine 'word'. In his reflection on this, man should consider the utter futility of allowing himself to become attracted to desires and lusts existing in 'worlds' so insignificant as to have been brought into being by but a single word. Far better for man to become attached to God Himself, higher than all worlds, to cleave to the essential rather than the subsidiary.[15]

Tzimtzum, it is here pointed out, is a continuous process and not one which took place once and for all. How, it is asked, can God have compassion for man? How can material things be contained at all in His most elevated thought? It can only be as a result of *Tzimtzum*. It is for this reason that the Hebrew word for 'matter'—*homer*—has the same letters as the word for 'compassion'—*rahum*. Since the relationship between God and man is a reciprocal one, the continuation of the *Tzimtzum* process (producing compassion) depends on man himself showing compassion. This is the mystical significance of the idea of *Imitatio Dei*—'Just as He is compassionate be thou compassionate'.[16] In another passage in this work it is stated that God's love is in exile in the garments it assumes in the material world. Therefore, for man to love a woman or food for themselves, without reference to their origin in the divine love, is to strip God of His garments.[17]

The psychological implications of *Tzimtzum* are similarly stressed by the great-grandson of the *Besht*, Nahman of Bratzlav (1772–1811). Were it not for God's withdrawal from his soul, there could be no consciousness for man, his whole being would have been engulfed in the splendour of the divine light, and all thought and action, and hence the recognition of God, would have been impossible. But just as in the cosmos God's sustaining power is provided by the ray of infinite light which penetrates the 'Empty Space' so, too, in man's soul. There is a reciprocal relationship between God and man. If man fills the vacuum in his soul with the ray of infinite light provided by godly thoughts, he causes the process to continue in the cosmos. He brings, as it were, God back into the space He has vacated. But if man fills his soul with evil thoughts, then God is kept out and an abyss is formed between God and His creation.[18]

Nahman even uses the *Tzimtzum* doctrine to defend the various controversies between rival Hasidic leaders, of which there were no lack and in which he himself was frequently involved.[19] The acrimonious debates between the *Tzaddiqim*, the Hasidic masters, are not only blameless, declares Nahman, but are necessary, if the world is to endure. A world without such controversies would resemble the state in which there is only the light of *'En Soph*. By their fierce divisions the *Tzaddiqim* help to create the 'empty space' without which there could be no finite world. A world without strife would be a world in which the light of *'En Soph* shines without *Tzimtzum* and this would be no separate world at all. Since their controversies, Nahman charitably observes, always concern spiritual matters, the *Tzaddiqim* cause the ray of divine light to penetrate the empty space they themselves have brought about by their quarrels. Only in this way can there be the creative ebb and flow. Just as God created the 'Empty Space' by His word so, too, do the *Tzaddiqim* take part in the act of creation by their words.[20]

According to Nahman, God is outside the time process altogether, hence *Tzimtzum* is not an event in far-off time, but takes place in the 'eternal Now'. Nahman's illustration of the dreamer is of great interest. In the dream, the barriers of space and time are removed. It is a common experience for many years and days to be telescoped in a dream into the compass of a few minutes or seconds. But when the dreamer awakes, his conscious mind becomes aware that the lengthy span of time in the dream was an illusion. For an intellect higher than man's, the latter's waking life is like a dream and its apparent lengthy span equally illusory. For Infinite Mind the time process is itself an illusion.[21]

It is, however, in *Ḥabad* thought that the latent ideas contained in earlier Hasidic sayings and teachings are developed in a fresh, systematic and vivid manner to yield what is virtually an original interpretation of some subtlety of the *Tzimtzum* idea.

NOTES TO CHAPTER THREE

[1] *V.* I. Broydé: 'Isaac ben Solomon Ashkenazi (*ARI*)' in *JE*, Vol. VIII, pp. 210–12; article 'Luria, Isaac' in *UJE*, Vol. 7, pp. 237–9; *Scholem: Major Trends, op. cit.*, pp. 244–86; I. Tishbi: *Torath Ha-Raʿ We-Ha-Qelipoth Be-Kabbalath Ha-ʾAri*, Jerusalem, 1942; S. A. Horodezky: *Torath Ha-Kabbalah Shel R. Yitzḥaq Luria*, Tel-Aviv, 1947.

[2] *V.* the full bibliography of Hayyim Vital's and other works on the Lurianic system in Scholem: *Major Trends, op. cit.*, pp 432–3

[3] *V.* the letter of R. Schneor Zalman regarding the Gaon's attitude in Dubnow: *Toledoth Ha-Ḥasiduth, op. cit.*, p. 253.

[4] The subject has been treated at length in M. Teitelbaum: *Ha-Rabh Mi-Ladi*, Vol. II, Warsaw, 1913, Chapters 1–3, pp. 37–94. I have followed Teitelbaum here, but comprehensive though his excellent account is, he has not noted sufficiently the views of the pre-*Ḥabad Ḥasidim* on the subject. The word *Tzimtzum*, it should be noted, is used of God in a number of Rabbinic Aggadic passages, e.g. *Midrash* Cant. R. to verse 1 : 14: 'The *Shekhinah* was concentrated (*metzumtzemeth*) between the two staves of the ark'; Lev. R. XXIX. 4: 'The Holy One, blessed be He, concentrates (*metzamtzem*) His *Shekhinah* among them below'. But in these Rabbinic sources the meaning is concentration into a point or place, whereas, in the Lurianic doctrine, the meaning is the exact opposite, withdrawal from a point or place. The root is the same, of course, in both meanings, but the use of the term in the sense of 'withdrawal' is original with Kabbalists, even though some of the latter quote the Rabbinic passages in support of their view, *v.* Teitelbaum, *op. cit.*, p. 47 note 2.

[5] *Shomer ʾEmunim*, Amsterdam, 1736, 'Second Discussion', *v.* Teitelbaum, *op. cit.*, pp. 48–49.

[6] *Mishnath Ḥasidim*, Amsterdam, 1727, Section on *Tzimtzum*, Chap. I; *Yosher Lebhabh*, Amsterdam, 1737, pp. 7–9; Teitelbaum, *op. cit.*, pp. 49–50.

[7] *Maggid Debharaw Le-Yaʿaqobh*, Koretz, 1784, p. 1a; *'Or Torah*, Lemberg, 1863, p. 1. These two are really the same work, containing Dobh Baer's ideas, but not written by him.

[8] *'Or Torah, Shir Ha-Shirim, s.v. mashekheni*.

[9] *'Or Torah*, p. 3. *Cf.* p. 5. It should be noted that occasionally Dobh Baer uses the term *Tzimtzum* in its Talmudic meaning of 'concentration' instead of 'withdrawal', e.g. when he says that God saw man's image before he was created and 'concentrated' on that image, *v. 'Or Torah*, p. 5. *Cf.* the same

work, *Wa-Yetze* beg., where Dobh Baer uses the illustration of a teacher who has to control the abundance of his wisdom and concentrate his mind on a very simple matter in order to convey this to the inferior intellect of his pupil. *Cf.* '*Or Torah*, *Shemoth*, where Dobh Baer elaborates on this theme and states that, in reality, *Tzimtzum* involves *both* concentration and withdrawal. When a man thinks on a certain matter, for instance, his mind is concentrated on the subject he contemplates and, at the same time, he withdraws from the contemplation of other matters.

[10] '*Or Torah*, *Wa-'Erah*. *Cf.* Dobh Baer's remarks *ibid.* that Moses, who was so small in his own eyes that he was as nothing, was able to encounter the divine *Nothing* without any screening. The same explanation regarding the 'sun' and the 'shield' is quoted in *Kether Shem Tobh*, Zolkiew, 1794–5, I, p. 28a.

[11] *Kether Shem Tobh*, *op. cit.*, I, p. 16. *Cf.* for the same thought II, p. 3, though here the *Tzimtzum* process is applied to *Binah*.

[12] *Kether Shem Tobh*, I, pp. 5a–b. The illustration of the 'snail' occurs in Gen. R. XXI, 5, but in an entirely different context. It appears that it was first applied to God in early Hasidism, but this requires further investigation. *Cf. Kether Shem Tobh*, I, p. 8b, that the meaning of the verse: 'Know this day, and lay it to thy heart, that the Lord He is God in heaven above and in the earth beneath; *there is none else*' (Deut. 4:39), is that, in reality, there is *nothing but God*, for otherwise the world would be 'separate' from '*En Soph* and this would imply limitation in God. This text became a favourite Ḥabad text.

[13] *Kether Shem Tobh*, I, pp. 53–54.

[14] Zolkiew, 1820.

[15] *Tzawwaath Ha-Ribhash*, p. 20.

[16] *Siphre* to Deut. xi.22, *Tzawwaath Ha-Ribhash*, p. 30.

[17] *Tzawwaath Ha-Ribhash*, p. 32, *cf.* pp. 35–36 that man should never fear any material things such as wild beasts since the source of that fear is in God. The same applies to man's love of material things.

[18] *Liqqute Moharan*, Ostrog, 1821, Part I, 49.

[19] *V.* Dubnow: : '*Toledoth Ha-Ḥasiduth*', *op. cit.*, pp. 304 f.

[20] *Liqqute Moharan*, Part II, 64.

[21] *Liqqute Moharan*, Part II, 61.

CHAPTER FOUR

Ḥabad

Ḥabad is the name given to the school of thought in Hasidism founded by Rabbi Schneor Zalman of Liady, disciple of the *Maggid* of Meseritch and teacher of Aaron. Before considering the particular interpretation given to the *Tzimtzum* doctrine by Ḥabad, it is as well to explain the precise significance of the name Ḥabad and its implications.

Ḥabad[1] is the intellectual movement in Hasidism, that tendency which sets great store by meditation and contemplation on the Kabbalistic themes. The term itself is derived from the initial letters of *Ḥokhmah* ('Wisdom'), *Binah* ('Understanding') and *Daʿath* ('Knowledge').[2] These three terms refer both to the Sephirotic realm and to those processes in man's psychic life in which that realm is mirrored. We have noted above that *Ḥokhmah* and *Binah* are the names of the second and third *Sephiroth*. *Daʿath* is a further principle in the Sephirotic realm by means of which *Ḥokhmah* and *Binah* are unified. In some Kabbalistic schemes *Daʿath* is counted as one of the *Sephiroth*, in which case *Kether* is elevated above the *Sephiroth* and is not counted among their number, thus preserving the essential number ten.

In Ḥabad thought each of these three terms has a precise definition. *Ḥokhmah* is wisdom in its potential stage. In the Sephirotic realm it is the divine thought of creation before the details have, as it were, become actualized in thought. In man's psychic life *Ḥokhmah* is the intuitive flash by which an idea emerges in the mind. Once the idea has come into being it becomes actualized through deep reflection—*Binah*—on its implications. When, as a result, the mind becomes powerfully attached to the idea it has grasped, when the idea becomes part of the person engaged in contemplation, *Daʿath* is attained.

A number of illustrations are given in the Ḥabad writings. When a man has the intention of giving charity or practising benevolence, the bare idea represents *Ḥokhmah*. *Binah* consists in reflection on the value of good works and on the concrete means of their realization. *Daʿath* represents the attachment of mind which precedes *Ḥokhmah* and *Binah* in man's basic interest in charity and which, at the same time, follows on them in terms of the firm resolve to implement the *Ḥokhmah* idea as actualized in *Binah*. Or an illustration can be given from aesthetic appreciation. *Ḥokhmah* is the bare notion of beauty which enables a man to see that a splendid building, for example, is truly beautiful. When he pauses to reflect on why he finds it beautiful, when he considers that his pleasure is caused by his appreciation of such things as the harmonious proportions and the skilful blending of colours, he attains to *Binah*. He now knows why he finds it beautiful. *Daʿath* is both the interest in beautiful things which moves him in the first place and the powerful attraction invoked by his reflections.[3]

Ḥabad is so called because the members of this group were expected to reflect deeply on the themes of divine transcendence and immanence, particularly as revealed in the *Ḥabad* interpretation of *Tzimtzum*. The basic idea of *Tzimtzum* is *Ḥokhmah*. Reflection on its detailed meaning is *Binah*. That special attachment of mind which both causes the devotee to be interested in the subject and which follows powerfully on contemplation is called *Daʿath*.

What is the novel *Ḥabad* interpretation of *Tzimtzum*?[4] It should be noted that Schneor Zalman, the founder of *Ḥabad*, claims that his ideas go back to the *Maggid* of Meseritch and the latter's son, Abraham the 'Angel', both of whom were Schneor Zalman's teachers in the *Kabbalah*.[5] From the examples quoted in the previous chapter it is clear that, indeed, Schneor Zalman had much to build on in the earlier Hasidic teachings. For all that, he has good claim to be considered the theoretician of Hasidism, the creator of a Hasidic metaphysical system. The difficulty Schneor Zalman faces is the apparent futility of the *Tzimtzum* doctrine in solving the problem of how there can be a world at all if God is all. If *Tzimtzum* really takes place, then there is limitation in God, since the world is not-God. If *Tzimtzum* does not take place, what does happen to produce the material world?

Schneor Zalman offers a solution remarkably reminiscent of Far Eastern religious thought. From God's point of view, as it were, *Tzimtzum* does not really take place. From His standpoint there is, indeed, no finite world, no 'upper world', no *Sephiroth* and no *Tzimtzum*. But from the point of view of creatures there is a world. This world is real enough from the creaturely standpoint, but it is unreal from God's point of view. *Tzimtzum* is not an actual withdrawal of God, but a screening of the divine light in order to enable creatures to exist in a finite world. It is a mistake to suggest that Ḥabad sees the physical universe as unreal to us and only as existing in God's thought, as an idea in the mind of God. In fact, the very opposite is true. So far as we are concerned, the universe is real enough. Ḥabad never discusses such matters as whether sense perception conveys a true picture of things as they are or the Kantian distinction between noumena and phenomena.[6] And, far from suggesting that the universe exists as an idea in God's mind, Ḥabad declares that finite creatures cannot talk at all about God's mind as it is in Itself.

Schneor Zalman is fond of developing an idea found, as we have seen, in the teachings of the *Maggid*. God is both a 'sun' and a 'shield'. The sun's rays are essential to life, but the sun must be 'shielded' if creatures are to endure its splendour. Here on earth, far from the sun, the rays enjoy an independent existence. But in the sun itself the rays become 'annihilated' (*bittul*, a favourite Ḥabad word) in the great light of the sun. Similarly, finite creatures only enjoy existence because the infinite divine light is screened. They can be compared to the rays of the sun, as they are on earth *apart* from the sun. But, in reality, the analogy is grossly inadequate, since the divine light is everywhere. From God's point of view, finite creatures are to be compared to the rays of the sun as they are *in the sun itself*, i.e. they enjoy no real independent existence.[7]

We have had occasion to note that the Kabbalistic name not alone for *'En Soph* but also for *Kether* is *'Ayin*, 'Nothingness', because nothing can be postulated, nothing grasped or comprehended, of God as He is in Himself. Creatures, on the other hand, inhabiting the world of sense perception, are called *yesh*, 'that which is'. Here, too, says Ḥabad a distinction must be drawn between the divine point of view and that of creatures. From our point of view God is "*ayin*', 'Nothingness', and finite beings '*yesh*', 'something'. But, in reality, from the ultimate and absolute standpoint of God, He is the true *yesh* and all His creatures are *'ayin*.⁸ The task of man in life is to pierce the veils by which the divine light is screened. By means of profound mediation and contemplation on the truth that all is in God, man loses himself completely in the divine 'Nothingness'. He becomes aware of the truth that there is, in reality, nothing but God. This stage of awareness is known as *bittul ha-yesh*, 'annihilation of somethingness', i.e. a losing of the self in God. Verses like *'Know this day, and lay it to thy heart, that the Lord, He is God in heaven above and upon the earth beneath; there is none else'* (Deut. 4:39) and *'Unto thee it was shown, that thou mightest know that the Lord, He is God; there is none else beside Him'* (Deut. 4:35) are interpreted in *Ḥabad* to yield the thought not only that there are no other gods or powers but that, in reality, there is only God.⁹ Similarly, the verse: *'The whole earth is full of His glory'* (Is. 6:3) is taken to mean not alone that God provides for all and extends His watchful care over all, but that He *is* all.

Ḥabad also develops an idea found in the writings of Hayyim Vital, and to some extent in earlier sources, that man has two souls.¹⁰ The first of these is known as the 'animal soul'—*nephesh ha-behamith*. This is the vital force in man by means of which he thinks, feels and acts. It is situated in the left ventricle of the heart, whence, by means of the blood stream, it extends to the whole of the body.¹¹ But, in addition, man has another soul which proceeds directly from God. This is the 'divine soul' —*nephesh ha-'elohuth*—and is seated in the brain, whence it extends to the whole of the body. The 'animal soul' is derived from the *Qelipah* ('shell' or 'husk', the evil surrounding the good as the bark the tree), known as *Nogah*, 'light'. According to the *Kabbalah*, the vision of the divine chariot in the opening chapter of the book of Ezekiel refers to four 'Shells' or '*Qelipoth*'. These are mentioned in the verse: 'And I looked, and, behold, a *stormy wind* came out of the north, a *great cloud*, with a *fire flashing up*, so that a *brightness* (*nogah*) was round about it' (Ez. 1:4).

The first three *Qelipoth* mentioned are entirely evil, but the *Qelipah* of *Nogah* contains a mixture of good and evil. Since the 'animal soul' is derived from *Nogah*, it follows that in all that man does under its power there is a mixture of good and evil. All man's thoughts, emotions and acts are tainted by the self-awareness and self-centredness conditioned by his animal soul.

This is the *Habad* version of original sin. But man has, too, a 'divine soul'. This—and here is the most radical of the *Habad* teachings—is an actual portion of *'En Soph*. It is truly a divine 'spark' in man.[12] This divine soul descends to earth in order to help man purge and purify his animal soul through his acknowledgement of God. Aided in this way, he is capable of transcending the consciousness of *yesh*, produced inevitably by the animal soul, and rise to its annihilation in God. The divine soul ever yearns for her Source in *'En Soph*, and in rising pulls the animal soul up with her. It must be said that *Habad* interprets all this as applying only to Jews. These have the divine soul given to them in the merit of the Patriarchs who followed God. It is God's precious gift to them through no merit of their own.

Non-Jews, with the exception of the 'righteous among the nations of the world', not only have no 'divine soul', but even their 'animal soul' derives not from *Nogah*, but from the three totally unclean *Qelipoth*. This doctrine was justly found to be a source of offence. It was one of the counts against Hasidism in the early polemics against the sect. Although Schneor Zalman is said to have argued that his views applied only to the pagans of old, it does appear from a detailed examination of his writings that he was speaking with his tongue in his cheek.[13] '*For a portion of the Lord is His people*' (Deut. 32:9) is taken by *Habad* to mean that in each Jew, deep in concealment, there is an actual *portion* of God.

To round off the picture, it would probably be helpful to quote some of the passages in the *Habad* writings, in which these ideas receive fairly full treatment.

Schneor Zalman, in his '*Tanya*',[14] attacks the Deist philosophy, in which creation is compared to the manufacture of an article such as a watch by a human craftsman. Once God has brought the universe into being, it is argued, His constant care and providence is no longer required, just as the watch continues to function without the watchmaker. But the great error here, observes Schneor Zalman, lies in the comparison of human activity with divine. No human creativity is *creatio ex nihilo*. Neither the watch itself nor its complicated mechanism are really created. The watchmaker simply puts the parts together so that they will function adequately. But the universe is created *ex nihilo* by God. This is a great marvel (*pele'*—we shall see that Aaron develops in detail this notion of *pele'*.) as a result of which the power of the Creator holds the universe suspended over the void. Were God's power to be withheld even for a moment, the whole universe would revert to the nothingness whence it emerged.

An illustration is given from the miraculous parting of the waters of the Red Sea, when Israel crossed on the dry land in the midst of the waters. The waters on either side stood firm like a wall solely through God's miraculous power. No sooner was that power removed than the waters returned to their natural state. The 'nature' of all created things is to revert to the nothingness whence they came. They are kept back from this only by God's power, which sustains them in their finite state. Thus, the true *Ḥasid* sees no world at all, only the divine 'Nothingness' which endows the finite world with the appearance of existence through successive screenings of the divine light.

In another passage the following idea of Schneor Zalman is recorded.[15] On the New Year festival God is entreated to 'remember' His world. The idea of remembrance can apply only to that which is not present. I can 'remember' a friend I have not seen for some time, not one who is facing me at this moment. Since the universe is ever-present to God, how can He be said to 'remember' it? The answer given is that from God's point of view there is no world at all. Consequently, it is not *really* present and God can be entreated to 'remember' it, i.e. to 'recall', as it were, the 'moment' in which He brought the world into being and to have compassion on His creatures.

Discussing the unity of God as taught in the *Shema'*, Israel's declaration of faith: '*Hear, O Israel, The Lord our God, the Lord is One*' (Deut. 6:4), Rabbi Menahem Mendel of Lübavitch, Schneor Zalman's grandson and the third leader of *Ḥabad*, observes[16] that there have been three interpretations of the idea of unity. The earliest and simplest idea is that there are no other gods. The *Shema'* is read as a simple declaration of monotheism. But during the Middle Ages the Jewish thinkers deepened this idea to include the meaning of God's uniqueness. In this view the *Shema'* declares not only that God is one, but that He can be compared to nothing in heaven and earth, that His true nature is known to none but Himself.

The third meaning, involving an even deeper refinement, is that given by the *Baʿal Shem Tobh* and his disciples, particularly the *Maggid* of Meseritch. According to this interpretation, God's unity means not alone His oneness and His uniqueness but that he is *all that there is*. God is one means that, in spite of all the evidence of diversity and compositeness in the universe, there is in the universe, in reality, only God's simple unity, i.e. from His point of view, there is no finite universe. 'That there is no reality in created things. This is to say that in truth all creatures are not in the category of "something" (*yesh*) or a "thing" (*dabhar*) as we see them with our eyes. For this is only from our point of view, since we are incapable of perceiving the divine vitality. But from the point of view of the divine vitality which sustains us, we have no existence and we are in the category of complete "nothingness" (*'ephes*), like the rays of the sun in the sun itself. . . . From which it follows that there is no other existence whatsoever, apart from God's existence, blessed be He. This is true unification. As the saying has it: "Thou art before the world was created and now that it is created"—in exactly the same manner. That is to say, just as there was no existence apart from God before the world was created so it is even now.'

The *Ḥasid* is expected to meditate long and thoroughly on the idea that all is in God. As a result of profound meditation on this theme, man's love can awaken to the extent that he has no will but for God. It is said that Schneor Zalman was once overheard saying: 'I do not desire Thy Paradise. I do not want Thy *Gan ʿEden*. I want Thee alone.'[17] This is said to be the meaning of the verse: 'Whom have I in heaven but Thee? And beside Thee I desire none upon earth' (Ps. 73:25), i.e. neither spiritual ('heaven') nor material ('earth') delights are of any significance compared with the love of God. Consequently, 'My flesh and my heart faileth' (Ps. 73:26) in the desire to become annihilated before Him and to cleave to Him.[18]

For *Ḥabad*, the virtue of humility does not mean that man thinks little of himself, but that he does not think of himself at all. Since from God's point of view there are no finite creatures man, by means of deep reflection on this theme, can learn to see himself as 'nothing'. This is the mystical Hasidic ideal of *bittul ha-yesh*, 'self-annihilation', 'nullification of the something'. This ideal has succeeded in producing among the *Ḥasidim* a spirit of confidence and indifference to the opinion of others. The *Ḥasid* is serene in his trust in God. He is neither grieved nor disturbed by anything which may befall him in the material world, for this exists for him only as the means of seeing through to the divine light. He strives to avoid any anxiety over his lack of success in worldly matters.

This is not to say that the *Ḥasid* is never sad or melancholy. Indeed, no one can be a true *Ḥasid* unless he is not too sanguine about his spiritual progress. He must always feel bitter about his remoteness from God.[19] Joy and sorrow are part of man's profoundest mystical experiences, joy at the tremendous possibility of seeing God in all and drawing near to Him, and sorrow at his remoteness from God. This Hasidic ideal was frequently criticized by those who saw in it the danger of complete indifference to wordly concerns. Quietism is perhaps a natural philosophy for some mystical minds, but in Hasidic circles it did at times provide an escape from responsibility.[20]

Ḥabad does not teach that it is really possible, while in the body, for man to see that all is nothing before God. In this life it is only through severe contemplation that one can arrive at that awareness of truth suggested by the term 'self-annihilation'. As Schneor Zalman remarks:[21] 'Every creature, every "something", is, in truth, as real "nothingness' in relation to the power of the Maker and the spirit of His mouth in His work, which enables it to exist continuously and causes it to emerge from real nothingness in somethingness. The reason every creature and object appears to us as something real and tangible is because we cannot see God's power and the spirit of His mouth in creatures with our eyes of flesh.

'But if the eye had been permitted to see and comprehend the vitality and spirituality in each creature, which flows from the utterance of God's mouth and the spirit of His mouth, the material nature of the creature, its physical substance and its tangibility would not be seen at all with our eyes. For the material nature is really cancelled out of existence in relation to the spirituality and vitality that is in it, since, apart from these, it would be nothing at all, as it actually was before the days of creation. It is the spirituality which comes from the utterance of God's mouth and the spirit of His mouth, which alone causes it to emerge from the void and from nothingness, so that it becomes something, and which allows it to exist. Since this is so there is, in reality, nothing else apart from Him.'

In our sketch of the *Ḥabad* doctrines we have used the terms 'from our point of view' and 'from God's point of view'. These terms, as we shall see, are used by Aaron Ha-Levi, but Schneor Zalman generally prefers to express the same distinction in different words. Basing himself on a term found in the Lurianic *Kabbalah*, Schneor Zalman refers to two kinds of divine light—'surrounding light' (*'or maqiph*) and 'clothed light' (*'or mithlabhesh*).[22] 'Surrounding light' is the sustaining power of *'En Soph* in all creatures. This is said to 'surround' creatures, in the sense that it cannot be seen by the eyes of flesh. It is the true source of creaturely existence and, in reality, is all that exists. But when this power is revealed through and in separate creatures it is called 'clothed light', i.e. the light of *'En Soph* as revealed in particular, finite things. Of course, there remains the difficulty of how the light of *'En Soph*, which cannot be grasped, becomes revealed, of how the 'surrounding light' becomes 'clothed light', but this is the general problem which *Ḥabad* has to face of how there can be a world from our point of view if there is no world from God's point of view. We shall have occasion to see later how Aaron tries to grapple with this problem. Schneor Zalman himself rarely takes up this basic question. Here, as well as in other areas, lies Aaron's originality, despite his disclaimers.

In Schneor Zalman's teachings, the Tetragrammaton, with its root meaning of 'being', denotes that God sustains all things and that all is in Him. One of the meanings of this divine name is said to be that God is above both Time and Space, for He gives 'being' to all that is in Space and to Space itself and, as for Time, He 'was, is and will be' all 'at once'.[23] Time and Space and the finite creatures which inhabit these are brought into being by that screening of the divine light known as *Tzimtzum*. This screening, this aspect of God's creative activity, is represented by the divine name *'Elohim* ('God'), suggesting 'restriction', 'judgement', 'limitation'.[24] Drawing on earlier sources, Schneor Zalman observes that the numerical value of the Hebrew word for 'nature' (*ha-tebha'*) is the same as that of

'*Elohim*.²⁵ When we speak of God as '*Elohim* we refer to God as manifested in nature. But nature is not really 'there' at all. Only God is true Reality.

When the *Kabbalah* refers to God as 'surrounding all worlds' as well as 'filling all worlds', the reference is to spiritual not to spatial transcendence. God is not outside Space and Time, for in reality there is no Space and Time. These are only brought about by that screening of the divine light we call *Tzimtzum*. The nearest we can get to the idea of divine transcendence and immanence is to use the analogy of thought in the human mind. To speak of an idea grasped in the mind as 'surrounded' by the mind is to convey the thought of one entity (the mind) being both transcendent and immanent in relation to another entity (the idea).²⁶ For all that, the analogy is far from adequate, since in *Ḥabad* thought the finite world does not really exist at all from God's point of view, whereas the mind and the idea it encompasses are two distinct entities.

The above are the main *Ḥabad* ideas upon which Aaron Ha-Levi's system is built. We turn now to a detailed examination of this system during which we shall have the opportunity of noting the special emphases introduced by him. It might be noted here that Aaron is the only one of the great *Ḥabad* masters to present his ideas in the form of a complete metaphysical system. Schneor Zalman himself is, to be sure, systematic, but not in the manner of Aaron, who presents his teachings in an almost mathematical progression. For this alone, quite apart from much that is original in his treatment of *Ḥabad* themes, Aaron has claims on our attention as an important acosmic thinker.

NOTES TO CHAPTER FOUR

¹ A full bibliography of Ḥabad is given by A. M. Habermann in the Jubilee Volume for Salman Schocken, Jerusalem 1952, pp. 293–370. A bibliography covering the writings of the official Ḥabad leaders down to the present is given in E. Steinmann's *Mishnath Ḥabad*, Tel-Aviv (n.d.), Vol. II, pp. 374–99. Steinmann's is a well-written, popular account of the movement, but sources are rarely given. There is much confusion between earlier and later ideas, and the work lacks an adequate historical and critical perspective. There are three biographies of Schneor Zalman: M. Teitelbaum's *Ha-Rabh Mi-Ladi U-Miphlegeth Ḥabad*, Vol. I, Warsaw, 1910, Vol. II, Warsaw, 1913; M. L. Rodkinsohn's *Toledoth ʿAmude Ḥabad*, Königsberg, 1876; H. M. Hielmann's *Beth Rabbi*, Berditchev, 1903, Yiddish version (less comprehensive), Vilna, 1904. Rodkinsohn's work is brief and distorted by hero-worship. Heilmann's work suffers from similar distortion, but contains a large amount of fairly reliable material handed down in the form of family traditions. (Heilmann belonged to the Schneorsohn family, the descendants of Schneor Zalman.) Teitelbaum's book is an effective account of both the life and thought of the Ḥabad founder. H. I. Bunim's *Mishneh Ḥabad*, Warsaw, 1936, is an excellent account of the movement, but here, too, Ḥabad thought is treated as a unity and little attempt is made to distinguish between the views of different teachers. *Cf.* Bunim's articles on Ḥabad in *Ha-Shiloaḥ*, Vol. XXVIII (1913), pp. 250–8, 348–59; Vol. XXIX (1913), pp. 217–27; Vol. XXXI (1914–15), pp. 44–52, 242–52. A complete collection of the letters of Schneor Zalman, together with other relevant documentary material, has been published by D. Z. Hillmann: *'Iggroth Baʿal Ha-Tanya*, Jerusalem, 1953. My translation of Dobh Baer's *Qunteros Ha-Hithpaʿaluth* ('Tract on Ecstasy'), Vallentine, Mitchell, London, 1963, is an account of the thinking of Schneor Zalman's son and successor and the rival of Aaron Ha-Levi.

² According to Rodkinsohn, *op. cit.*, p. 7 note 7, the name Ḥabad was not used for the movement until the time of Dobh Baer, and was derived from the substitution of the words Ḥokhmah, Binah Wa-Daʿath for Deʿah Binah We-Haskel in the daily service. But this is incorrect. In a letter to Abraham of Kalisk (D. Z. Hillmann, *op. cit.*, p. 176) Schneor Zalman himself refers to his group as Ḥabad.

³ Schneor Zalman defines Ḥokhmah, Binah and Daʿath in his *Tanya*, Vilna, 1930, Chapter III, pp. 13–14. The definitions given in the text are those of Hillel ben Meir of Parits in his *Liqqute Biʾurim*, Warsaw, 1868, Part II, Commentary on Dobh Baer's *Shaʿar Ha-Yiḥud*.

⁴ *V*. in particular Bunim: *Mishneh Ḥabad*, *op. cit.*, and Teitelbaum, *op. cit.*, Vol. II, Chap. 3 and 4, pp. 62–120.

⁵ *V*. Hielmann, '*Beth Rabbi*', *op. cit.*, Part I, pp. 81–90. Schneor Zalman's

own name for the *Tanya* was *Liqqute 'Amarim*, 'Collected Sayings', with the statement in the subtitle that the teachings recorded had been garnered from his teachers.

⁶ It is a major fault of Teitelbaum's otherwise excellent work (*v.* particularly Vol. II, pp. 97 f.) that he fails to see this point. Dubnow: *Toledoth Ha-Ḥasiduth, op. cit.*, pp. 234–5, is similarly confused in referring to Berkeley, Hume and Kant in connection with Schneor Zalman's ideas.

⁷ *Tanya, Shaʿar Ha-Yiḥud We-Ha-'Emunah*, Chap. 3–4, pp. 155–8.

⁸ *V. Liqqute Torah*, Gen., Vilna, 1884, p. 2; Deut., Vilna, 1878, *Shir*, p. 64; *Tanya, 'Iggereth Ha-Qodesh*, 20, p. 258; Bunim: *Mishneh Ḥabad, op. cit.*, Chap. IV, pp. 104–35.

⁹ *V. Tanya, Shaʿar Ha-Yiḥud We-Ha-'Emunah*, Chap. I, p. 152 f.

¹⁰ *V.* Hillel Zeitlin: *Maphteaḥ Le-Sepher Ha-Zohar* in *Ha-Tequphah*, Vol. IX, Warsaw, 1921, pp. 287 f.; Hayyim Vital: *Shaʿare Qedushah*, Sulzbach, 1748, Part I; *Tanya*, Part I, Chap. 1–2, pp. 9–13; *Liqqute Torah*, Deut., Vilna, 1878, pp. 75–76.

¹¹ *Tanya*, Part I, Chap. 9, pp. 26 f.

¹² *V. Tanya*, Part I, Chap. 9, pp. 26 f.; David Baumgardt: *Great Western Mystics*, Columbia University Press, New York, 1961, pp. 82–83.

¹³ *V.* Dubnow, *op. cit.*, p. 236.

¹⁴ *Shaʿar Ha-Yiḥud We-Ha-'Emunah*, Chap. 2, pp. 153–4.

¹⁵ *Liqqute Torah*, Deut., Vilna, 1878, *Derushim Le-Rosh Ha-Shanah*, p. 116.

¹⁶ *Sepher Derekh Mitzwothekha*, Poltava, 1911, p. 123.

¹⁷ M. Buber: *Tales of the Hasidim*, Schocken Books, Vol. I, New York, 1947, p. 267.

¹⁸ *Liqqute Torah*, Num., Zhitomer, 1866, p. 59.

¹⁹ *V.* Dobh Baer's *Qunteros Ha-Hithpaʿaluth*, ed. Warsaw (under title: *Liqqute Bi'urim*), 1868, pp. 59b–60a, in my translation, *op. cit.*, pp. 148–9.

²⁰ *V.* e.g., Dubnow, *op. cit.*, pp. 349–54.

²¹ *Tanya, Shaʿar Ha-Yiḥud We-Ha-'Emunah*, Chap. 3, p. 155.

NOTES

[22] *V.* Teitelbaum, *op. cit.*, Vol. I, pp. 71 f.

[23] *Tanya, Shaʿar Ha-Yiḥud We-Ha-'Emunah*, Chap. 7, p. 163.

[24] *Liqqute Torah*, Gen., Vilna, 1884, Comment on Gen. 2:18, p. 52.

[25] *Tanya, Shaʿar Ha-Yiḥud We-Ha-'Emunah*, Chap. 6, pp. 159–62, *cf.* Teitelbaum, *op. cit.*, Vol. II, pp. 119–20, for this equation between 'God' and 'nature'.

[26] *V. Tanya*, Part I, Chap. 51, pp. 141–4. *Cf.* Chap. 5, pp. 17–19.

CHAPTER FIVE

Rabbi Aaron's Method

In his Introduction to *Shaʿare Ha-Yiḥud We-Ha-'Emunah*, Aaron, like many of his Kabbalistic predecessors, seeks to justify his systematic presentation of the Kabbalistic mysteries in a manner which all can read. The earlier teachers frowned on any attempt at revealing these mysteries to the uninitiated. The *Kabbalah* is esoteric wisdom, yet Aaron, following the general Ḥabad attitude, is bent on a detailed exposition of the secret lore for the ordinary reader. The very title of the Introduction is *Pethaḥ U-Mabho Ha-Sheʿarim* ('Door and Introduction to the Gates'). Aaron is aware, and seeks justification for so doing, that he is opening a door which the earlier masters had declared closed.[1]

Aaron begins his apologia by quoting from earlier Kabbalists who wrote similar introductory works. Cordovero's *'Or Neʿ-erabh* is devoted to the advocacy of Kabbalistic studies and is a general introduction to these. Indeed, remarks Aaron, this type of study is essential to the religious life, since the whole purpose of divine worship is 'to unite the Holy One, Blessed be He, with His *Shekhinah*', and there can be no true unification if knowledge is lacking. But the paradox here is that, for all its praiseworthiness, the knowledge of God is not possible for the finite human mind.

The *Kabbalah* offers the way out of the dilemma. God, it is true, is incomprehensible, but the traditional Kabbalistic wisdom affords us knowledge of those aspects of His nature (including the knowledge that as He is in Himself He is incomprehensible) we need to have if we are to realize the unification. Thus, the knowledge of God is not speculative. It cannot be attained by unaided human reason. It is revealed knowledge; the ancient wisdom of the *Kabbalah* being partly revealed by God to Moses on Sinai and partly taught by Elijah to those worthy of being the recipients of the truth. Knowledge of God, then, means contemplation of the revealed Kabbalistic mysteries. It follows that Kabbalistic studies cannot be entirely proscribed, since without them there can be no knowledge of

God and hence no unification and no divine worship. What, then, is the meaning of the older prohibition of this study, except for the few initiates? A distinction must be made between the basic degree of knowledge required for divine worship to be effective, and a more profound, detailed esoteric gnosis. The former, far from being forbidden, is enjoined upon every Jew. The latter is for the aristocrats of the spirit. It is the former knowledge which Aaron seeks to describe in his work.

Furthermore, argues Aaron, without the knowledge of God, there can be neither love nor fear of Him. One can only love or fear that which one sees. In the nature of the case this is impossible with regard to God, but knowledge of Him is equivalent to 'seeing' Him. As Aaron puts it: 'Love of God and attachment (*debhequth*) to Him are unimaginable without the knowledge of His unity, Blessed be He. For the idea of love can only apply to a being of which one has knowledge and recognises, so that one becomes joined to the being one knows. *A fortiori*, attachment can only be conceived of as a complete bond by means of which two become as one. How then can the idea of love be applied to God, Blessed be He, whose being is unknown and can in no way be comprehended? *A fortiori*, how can the term "attachment" be applied to That which is beyond all thought and comprehension? On the contrary, one is dealing with two opposites, since God, Blessed be He, is infinite while the worlds and man are finite. So, too, the idea of inner fear—namely, to stand abashed at God's greatness, Blessed be He—can only be applied to something one sees.

'For instance, one who stands in the king's presence to witness his greatness feels so abashed that he loses his own identity, but one who knows the king only by repute feels no shame and suffers no loss of identity. He will fear the king's punishments and decrees, but will experience no sense of shame or loss of identity if the king is remote from him. This is axiomatic to every intelligent person and it is for this reason that the letters of the word "fear" (*yirah*) and the word "sight" (*re'eyah*) are the same. It follows that man can only attain to inner fear—in which he stands abashed before God and loses his identity completely in annihilation before Him—through comprehension of God's unity, Blessed be He, in the worlds. This means the knowledge that there is none but God and that, in reality, all things are as naught before Him, that, apart from Him, there is nothing at all and that all the worlds are not things separate from His being, God forfend.

As a result of this contemplation of God's unity, awe and dread will seize man so that he stands abashed before God's greatness, Blessed be He, and he annihilates his "somethingness" (which only appears as a "something" and as a separate thing) and loses himself in God's unity.' It is for this reason, concludes Aaron, that in the *Shemaʿ*, Israel's declaration of faith (Deut. 6:4–5), the command to love God is preceded by the declaration of God's unity. When Israel 'hears' (=understands) that God is one, Israel loves God.

Interpreting the mystical ideal of the unification of the Holy One, Blessed be He, and His *Shekhinah*, Aaron explains that the former term refers to God as He is in Himself, while the term *Shekhinah* means God as He is revealed in the worlds in which He dwells (from *shakhan*, 'to dwell'). From the point of view of God's revelation to us, these two aspects of the Deity are in complete contradiction, for God's essence is beyond all limit and comprehension, whereas the worlds *appear* as finite and in separation from Him. By means of Israel's worship and the resulting unification the Holy One, Blessed be He, and His *Shekhinah* become, as it were, united, i.e. the appearance of separateness which the finite world enjoys is transcended so that the truth is seen that, in reality, all is God.

Aaron acknowledges that what he calls 'natural love and fear', i.e. the love and fear which stem from simple faith in God's unity, also constitute perfect worship. But the love and fear which stem from contemplation of God's unity are far more elevated. Nor must one think in terms of two entirely different persons, the man of simple faith and the mystical adept. Since there is an ebb and flow in the life of faith, every man has his spiritual ups and downs. There are times when man can attain to the higher unification by means of severe contemplation, and there are other times when all he can do is to fall back on simple faith.

Thus, on the basis of his thesis that Kabbalistic wisdom is indispensable for the love and fear of God, Aaron, following his master, draws a distinction between two parts of the ancient mystic lore. That part which concerns the knowledge that all is in God is essential to proper worship. Far from there being any ban on this kind of knowledge, it must be studied and mastered by every Jew. It is the more esoteric mysteries, dealing with such matters as the correct combination of the divine names, the description of the heavenly chariot, the ineffable name of God, and the detailed magical effort to influence the upper worlds, that is reserved for the initiate and forbidden to others.

Historically considered, the distinction is, of course, artificial. It reflects rather the situation in Aaron's time. *Ḥabad* is hardly interested at all in the practical side of Kabbalism, but it is intensely interested in the theosophical doctrines of the *Kabbalah*. There can be little doubt that when the earlier teachers placed a ban on Kabbalistic study it applied to this theosophical knowledge as well as to the practical *Kabbalah*. Aaron and the other *Ḥabad* leaders, however, feel themselves called upon to justify the new emphasis in Hasidism on the popular teaching of the divine mysteries, and this they do by seeing them as the only aid to real love and fear of God. For them, the *Kabbalah* is no longer a matter of miracle working, but a metaphysical system of revealed truth about the nature of God and His relationship to man and the world.

It should, however, be noted that Aaron is not entirely unaware that much of this is new and due to the different emphasis required by Hasidism. In the language of the *Kabbalah*, Aaron states that he had heard from his master (Schneor Zalman), who in turn heard it from his master (the *Maggid* of Meseritch), who heard it from his master (the *Ba'al Shem Tobh*), that these generations, which belong to the 'heel' aspect (unlike earlier generations which belonged to the 'head' or other parts of the body), are quite different in their spiritual organization.

In former times souls were completely divided among men according to the roots of the particular soul in Heaven. The souls which came from the World of Creation (*'Olam Ha-Beriah*) were, on earth, the Rabbis and their disciples. The souls which came from the World of Formation (*'Olam Ha-Yetzirah*) were, on earth, the merchants who supported the *Torah* students. The souls which came from the World of Action (*'Olam Ha-'Asiyah*) were, on earth, the ignorant masses. But nowadays there is a mixture of souls, so that no person on earth has one specific manner of worship which applies particularly to him. At times a man is nowadays moved to serve God in one way, at times in another. Hence the way of contemplation is possible for all men some of the time, while the way of simple faith is open to them all when contemplation seems to them a remote ideal.

Arguing further for the popularization of Kabbalistic studies, Aaron goes beyond his earlier distinction between the two aspects of these studies. Nowadays, he remarks, the whole area of the *Kabbalah* should be open ground, since, in our poverty of good deeds, the mystical lore is the only shield we possess. In former times, when the initiates could really attain to the full knowledge of the esoteric wisdom, there was point to the distinction. Nowadays, when, in any event, true adepts are so few as to be negligible, all can and should engage in this study. In this connection, Aaron quotes a parable of Schneor Zalman. A king normally gives the keys of the rooms in his palace to various princes. This prince has the key to one room, that prince to another. No prince is allowed to use another's key in order to gain access to a room forbidden to him. But when the palace is thrown open for inspection by the masses, these are allowed to enter all the rooms of the palace, since, in any event, the normal rules are suspended.

This is the difference between earlier generations and our own. In former times each devotee had his own special insight, his own way to the divine mysteries, the keys to open his particular door in the palace of the divine mysteries. But nowadays, when there are no keys, when no one can really penetrate to the true meaning of the more esoteric side of Kabbalism, the palace doors are thrown open to all. Now all can wander freely about the mystical palace, not as princes but as sightseers who wish to become lost in wonder at the glory, i.e., who desire no more than to attain to self-annihilation (*bittul ha-yesh*) before God's splendour. Furthermore, in former ages the saints were so near to God that it became necessary to keep them at a distance if they were not to be blinded by the tremendous light. But there is no danger of this nowadays. On the contrary, so remote are we that only the greater light can equip us to have any vision at all.

Aaron goes on to refer to a Talmudic passage[2] in which it is said that Isaiah was like a townsman who had seen the king. As a result of his familiarity, his description is brief (Is. 6), whereas Ezekiel was like a villager who had seen the king, and to him it was all so unfamiliar that he gave a far lengthier description of what he had seen (Ez. 1). Nowadays, by the same token, lengthy works of Kabbalistic exposition, such as Aaron's own, are required, unnecessary though these were in ages of greater familiarity with the divine.

All this belongs to Aaron's defence of the unconventional nature of his enterprise. Finally, he observes, there are 'secret' reasons, belonging to the mysteries of divine providence, why Kabbalistic studies have become popular. This probably means that in these later ages, when the footsteps of the Messiah are heard, it is particularly necessary for men to pave the way for the Messiah by becoming conversant with the divine secrets.

Aaron then turns to the specific contribution made by Hasidism to Kabbalistic lore. He observes that, while there can be no doubt that the rich symbolism used by Luria and his disciple Hayyim Vital expressed the profoundest spiritual ideas, many later Kabbalists took these symbols in far too literal a fashion, with the result that God is spoken of by them in grossly material and corporeal terms. It was the task of the *Baʿal Shem Tobh* to restore the Lurianic *Kabbalah* to its original deeply spiritual and refined meaning. Elijah revealed himself to the *Baʿal Shem* and taught him the true inner meaning of the *Kabbalah*. The *Baʿal Shem* then revealed the secrets of this wisdom. He invented many parables, particularly of a psychological nature, believing as he did that the relationship between God and the world can best be described in terms of man's soul in its relation to his body.

In this connection, Aaron, like his medieval predecessors, quotes the verse in Job: 'From my flesh I behold God' (Job 19:26), i.e. God's relationship with the world can be understood from the way it is mirrored in man's psychic life.[3] The *Maggid* of Meseritch, in turn, invented further illustrations to make these difficult subjects more intelligible, and his disciple, Schneor Zalman, presented the whole subject in his expositions in a systematic manner. 'As my own eyes, and no stranger's, have seen while the sun shone upon earth the ideas were presented as joyfully as the day on which they were given on Sinai.' But on the death of the master all became dark again. Even though his writings are extant, these cannot always be correctly understood and, in this field, this is extremely unfortunate, since here human reasoning is powerless to fill the gaps. Only a disciple of many years' standing, such as Aaron himself, can interpret the master's teachings authentically.

In the field of Talmudic studies in his day, Aaron complains, while the sounder scholars have a proper grasp of the meaning, many prefer the involved subtleties of Talmudic dialectics—*pilpul*—and stray far from the true meaning of the *Talmud*. Among the Kabbalists, too, there are still to be found students of the 'plain meaning', but there are also many who have wandered far from the true path, so that it becomes absolutely essential for a clear, systematic presentation of the true ideas to be given. This Aaron sets out to do.

In this matter of using illustrations from the material universe to explain the intricacies of the *Kabbalah*, Aaron lays down certain basic rules. Although the *mashal*—the parable—may and should be used, three conditions must be fulfilled if it is to be effective. Nevertheless, he says, no parable can ever be exact. The analogy of the soul in the body, for instance, is helpful and is frequently used to convey the idea of God's relationship to the world, but it must not be pressed too far. It can serve as no more than a pointer to the truth. Aaron accepts a theology of analogy, but declares that for it to be legitimate these three conditions must be fulfilled.

The first condition is that the *mashal* must be based on the true *Kabbalah*, i.e. it must be found in the classic Kabbalistic sources or, at least, be based on something found there. As we have seen, Aaron believes these sources to contain revealed truth. The unaided human reason is utterly incapable of arriving at any knowledge of God and His relationship to the world. All human reasoning is tentative and uncertain. At best it can only arrive at *probable* conclusions. It can only fail utterly if it attempts to invent analogies with which to describe the Infinite. Only God Himself, as it were, can provide the requisite analogies, and this He has done through His revelation to the saints in the *Kabbalah*. Once, however, the basic analogy has been given, it is permitted for the human mind to elaborate on it.

The second condition limits the application of the *mashal* to the relationship between God and the world. The use of illustration is only legitimate if it is clearly understood as referring to God as He reveals Himself in creation. It must never be applied to God as He is in Himself, for of this aspect of the Deity nothing at all can be known and it cannot be grasped, even by means of a highly qualified analogy.

The third and most important condition of all is that the inadequacy of the *mashal* must always be kept in mind. No matter how illuminating the *mashal* appears to be, it must never be pressed too far and it must be clearly realized that, in reality, no illustration from the material universe can describe the Infinite. Thus, the analogy of the soul in the body is valid if the three conditions are fulfilled. The first is fulfilled, since this *mashal* is found in the classical sources. The second condition is satisfied if it is clearly understood that, even by analogy, the *mashal* does not purport to convey anything at all about God's unfathomable nature. As for the third condition, it must be realized that there is no actual point of resemblance between God in the world and the soul in the body. Soul and body are two distinct entities. From our point of view God is, indeed, apart from the world, and one can speak of Him and His *Sephiroth* as distinct from one another. But from His point of view He is one with His *Sephiroth*. The whole Sephirotic doctrine has relevance only to the worlds which the *Tzimtzum* process reveals. But from the standpoint of God there is only simple unity.

Unless the greatest care is taken to ensure that all three conditions are fulfilled, there is the utmost danger of ascribing some kind of corporeality to God or of thinking of Him in gross terms. Indeed, unless these conditions are fulfilled, it is better to avoid Kabbalistic study entirely. The simple believer, content to affirm the oneness of God without understanding its meaning, is, in this regard, in a far less perilous state than the inept Kabbalist who takes the anologies literally. The ultimate purpose of Kabbalistic study is, indeed, to know that we really do not know.

For this reason it is harmful to take Schneor Zalman's writings literally. Only a student who has sat for many years at the feet of the master is capable of penetrating to the true heart of his teaching. These three conditions, continues Aaron, are by no means his own invention, but were laid down by the master himself. If a passage in his writings appears to contradict one of the conditions, the fault can only be that of whoever recorded his words. Far from claiming originality, Aaron protests that it is all based on Schneor Zalman's ideas to which he, as a disciple, has merely added a more detailed exposition. Ultimately all these ideas are based on revealed truth higher than reason, even though the ideas themselves are extremely profound and are capable of invoking the admiration of the human intellect.

'All these ideas regarding the unity of God, Blessed be He, are based on faith which is higher than human reasoning. Although they are exceedingly profound matters which can be comprehended, yet none of them can be attained through the exercise of the unaided human mind, nor can they be at all comprehended by means of purely human ratiocination. For they are divine ideas, and just as God Himself, Blessed be He, is beyond all human intellect and knowledge so, too, whatever derives from Him in the world He has created and His unification with them cannot be grasped at all by human intellect and knowledge. The whole matter of comprehending these things belongs in the category of the marvellous. For all that, though they do not belong to comprehension by the human mind, they are to be expounded as powerful and profound ideas in relation to which all purely human ideas are as darkness to light and even more so. All these ideas are expounded by means of the most powerful proofs and demonstrations. When the discerning reader grasps the profundity of these expositions, the gates of light will be revealed to him.'

Aaron's insistence on the limitations of human reasoning in understanding the Kabbalistic mysteries, and his strict conditions to be observed when using the parable, are almost certainly aimed at his rival, Dobh Baer.

We know that contemporary Hasidic masters in Poland and Galicia were critical of Dobh Baer's expositions on the ground that they were too 'philosophical', relying too much on human reasoning. For instance, Rabbi Zewi Hirsch of Zhydatchov (d. 1831) quotes his teacher, Rabbi Yaakov Yitzhak of Lublin, the 'Seer' (d. 1815), as saying that an attempt to make the mysteries intelligible to the human mind is to corporealize the concepts, and that this borders on mystical heresy.[4] More explicitly. Rabbi Zewi Hirsch has this to say of Dobh Baer:[5] 'This is contrary to the printed work of a famous scholar of our day, who explained all this in a book called *Shaʿar Ha-Yiḥud*.[6] Brother, believe me that no light shines on any of his ways of human investigation and the use of parables, which have neither utility nor value. I have earlier advised thee, brother, to keep thyself remote from this. For all his ways here can be presumed to be dangerous, one who guards his soul will be far from them. God is my witness that I do not say this for my glory, but to keep my friends far from these investigations, in which there is a mixture of philosophy. And this is sufficient.'

The Polish and Galician *Ḥasidim* appear to have been generally suspicious of the intellectual approach of *Ḥabad*, but particularly of Dobh Baer's emphasis on human reasoning and his rather negative attitude towards religious emotion. Aaron, as a *Ḥabad* follower, does not go the whole way with them. We have seen how he, too, tends to agree with Dobh Baer that sham ecstasy is far from the ideal, but he is not as severe as Dobh Baer in rejecting it entirely. Similarly with regard to the use of human reasoning and analogy. He is unwilling to go all the way with Dobh Baer's opponents in rejecting every attempt to explain the mysteries in terms intelligible to the human mind. But at the same time, he cannot bring himself to agree with Dobh Baer that great licence can be given to pure human reasoning in this sphere. In Aaron's view the parable may be used, but it must be severely controlled on the lines he suggests.

It would thus seem that, in addition to their different approaches to the life of ecstasy, Dobh Baer and Aaron differ on the role of human reasoning in grasping the Kabbalistic mysteries. On both these issues Dobh Baer is radically at variance with the Polish and Galician *Ḥasidim*, with Aaron adopting a middle-of-the-road position.

Aaron states[7] that his two volumes—*Shaʿare Ha-Yiḥud We-Ha-'Emunah* and *Shaʿare ʿAbhodah*—are, in reality, one lengthy work of exposition of Schneor Zalman's *Tanya*, which is itself divided into two parts. Aaron prefers to divide the material into two separate books, the first dealing with God's unity, the second with the application of the theory in practice in prayer and worship. Although the chief value of the knowledge of God's unity is in its use in divine worship, yet this knowledge constitutes a science in itself, requiring a special volume for its detailed treatment.

Aaron is under no illusion as to the difficulty of his task. It requires, he says, profound study and application. It cannot possibly be understood from a superficial reading. Yet even the unlearned should not be deterred from perusing the work, even though full benefit from it will be obtained only by the expert prepared to devote much time and effort. 'Even those who do not understand it adequately will still benefit from this work in a general way. For in a general way they will come to appreciate that there is nothing else but God, Blessed be He, and that He is in all worlds and is united with them so that there is no place empty of Him. By means of this general appreciation they will attain to the love and fear of God, Blessed be He.' The reader is warned, however, against skipping passages, since the work has been arranged in careful stages, one axiom leading on to another.

Aaron adds two further notes for the reader. The first is that the purpose of the study of this work of his should be for the heart to be moved ecstatically in the love and fear of God, as a result of the deeper knowledge of God the work offers. There is no point at all, he says, in treating the subject like any other science and approaching it in a detached manner, calmly dispassionate. The sole justification for man to acquire a deeper knowledge of God is for the fruit of this to be garnered in richer worship. Moreover, this kind of knowledge is an art in which participation of the committed self is absolutely essential. A knowledge of how music is composed is far different from a real appreciation of music. 'Without sensation, self-involvement and emotional ecstasy this cannot be called knowledge at all, and there will be no benefit whatsoever, God forfend, from the study of this work.'

Aaron's second note calls the reader's attention to the need for engaging in the more conventional topics of *Torah* study, i.e. Bible, Talmud and the Codes. These, rather than the *Kabbalah*, should be man's staple spiritual diet. These form the bread of *Torah* without which one cannot exist.[8] Certainly Kabbalistic studies are meritorious, but they can only lead man part of the way. They can, as has been said, never enable him to comprehend God's essence. But in the study of the practical side of Judaism, in the study of the divine precepts (*mitzwoth*) and in their observance, man comes as near to God as is possible for humans in this life. For, as Schneor Zalman has stated in the *Tanya*,[9] the will of God as revealed in the divine commands is not something other than God Himself. Man himself is one entity, his will another. But God's will is not an entity separate from His essence. God *is* His will, so that it follows that when man studies that will and obeys it in practice he is, as it were, in the closest contact with God Himself. This alone is capable of nourishing the soul. Only here is God truly revealed, even in the material world.

On the other hand, bread can only nourish a living person, not a corpse. Hence the need for Kabbalistic studies. Reflection and sustained meditation on the divine mysteries move the heart in fear and love. They provide man with the spiritual energy and vitality he requires if the divine precepts are to have their effect. Thus, all Aaron's stress on the value of Kabbalistic studies is not intended to suggest that these are intrinsically more important than the more conventional studies engaged in by the devout Jew. On the contrary, the latter are the most important activity open to the Jew. *Kabbalah* is indispensable, but only because without it man's soul becomes so dead that ordinary *Torah* studies can have no effect upon him.

It is in the minutiae of observance that Aaron finds the supreme example of divine revelation. As Chesterton observed in speaking of the mystics: 'Little things please great minds.'[10] We have in all this, of course, an example of the tension in Hasidism between the claims of the conventional pattern of Jewish intellectual and spiritual life and those of the new interest in mysticism. *Ḥabad* tries to solve the problem not only by the intellectualization of mysticism but also by the mysticization of intellectualism. The study of the 'revealed things' becomes itself a mystical exercise of the first importance.

In conclusion, Aaron urges his followers to set aside periods for *Torah* study, both of the 'revealed things' and of the secret lore of the *Kabbalah*. Those blessed with a greater degree of intellectual capacity should help those less gifted to understand the profound topics dealt with in the work. Aaron apologizes for writing the work at all. That he has done so, he says, is not for the purpose of acquiring fame for himself, but solely in order to convey the truth regarding God's unity.

NOTES TO CHAPTER FIVE

[1] *SYE, Pethaḥ U-Mabho Ha-She'arim*, pp. 1a–13b. The text from here down to 'the gates of light will be revealed to him' on p. 85 is all based on this passage.

[2] *Ḥag.* 13b.

[3] For a very full treatment of this theme as it appears in the medieval literature v. Alexander Altmann: 'The Delphic Maxim in Medieval Islam and Judaism' in *Biblical and Other Studies*, ed. Alexander Altmann, Harvard University Press, 1963, pp. 196–232. *Cf.* Menahem G. Glenn: *Israel Salanter*, Bloch Publishing Co., New York, 1953, p. 167 note 16.

[4] *V.* Zewi Hirsch's *Sur Me-Ra' We-'Aseh Tobh*, Lemberg, 1858, edition used *Kether* (n.d.), p. 99: 'I have explained all this at great length because I have seen that the sages of our generation expound all the words of the *Zohar*, the *'Idroth* and the writings of the *'Ari*, which speak of the *Partzuphim*, and the Four Worlds, by saying that it is all in the nature of parable and riddles, containing the wisdom necessary for God's worship. They explain these matters by means of parables invented by the human mind and they remove the concepts from their true status, in order to bring them near to human reasoning.'

[5] Zewi Hirsch, *op. cit.*, p. 144 note.

[6] The *Sha'ar Ha-Yiḥud* ('Gate of Unity') was published by Dobh Baer during his lifetime as Part II of his *Ner Mitzwah We-Torah'Or*, Kopust, 1820. It was also printed as an appendix to Schneor Zalman's *Torah 'Or*, Lemberg, 1851, under the title *Qunteros Ha-Hithbonanuth*, 'Tract on Contemplation'.

[7] *SYE, ibid.*, pp. 14b–17a. The text to the end of this chapter is based on this passage.

[8] *V. Shulḥan 'Arukh, Yorek De'ah*, 246:4.

[9] *V. Tanya*, Vilna, 1930, Part I, Chap. 5, pp. 17–19, *Qunteros 'Aḥaron*, pp. 318–21.

[10] *The Man Who Was Orthodox—A Selection from the Uncollected Writings of G. K. Chesterton*, Arranged and Introduced by A. L. Maycock, Dennis Dobson, London, 1963, p. 165.

CHAPTER SIX

'En Soph *and The Universe*

Aaron is true to the idea found, as we have seen, in the *Zohar* and the writings of the later Kabbalists, that God as He is in Himself, *'En Soph*, is utterly beyond all human comprehension. Of *'En Soph* nothing at all can be postulated. When, for instance, we speak of God's wisdom, we mean that God is the source of all wisdom, that all wisdom derives from Him, but we must never speak as if a term like 'wisdom' can really be applied to God. We cannot even say that God's wisdom is too elevated to be comprehended by man, for this would imply that there is some point of resemblance and comparison between divine and human wisdom, a difference only in degree and not in kind.[1] The basic meaning of the *Kabbalah* here is that no attribute or quality can be ascribed to *'En Soph*. 'One has only to believe that all things are from Him, Blessed be He, and all creatures are to be seen as united in His unity but, God forfend, one must not think of any attribute or quality in relation to His essence, for on this depend all the main principles of authentic *Kabbalah* and the fundamental roots of unification and belief.'[2]

'En Soph is 'simple to the uttermost extent of simplicity' (*pashut be-takhlith ha-peshituth*). The meaning of this is that there is no compositeness in His nature. Created things are composite and consequently suffer change. Minerals, plants, animals and humans are all composed of the four elements, fire, air, water and earth. In another way, too, created things are composite. They have a body (i.e. the material thing itself) and a soul (i.e. the divine vitality by which a thing endures).

A further distinction must be drawn between the composite and the simple. Every creature has a composite nature, but each element of its composition is simple and non-composite. But the simplicity of the elements is only relative; they are simple in relation to the things they compose. But in themselves they, too, are composite, since in each there is something of the others. Water, for instance, has taste, which shows that it is not really simple. The soul of man, too, is composite. It reveals itself through the bodily organs in different ways, kindness, anger and the like. Only *'En Soph* is entirely without any compositeness whatsoever. No other forces or powers operate in Him. Aaron's objection to thinking of God as in any way composite is the general medieval refusal to accept the notion of anything as co-existing with God from all eternity. If there is anything else but God, even if this is a force or power in His own being, this would belong to His eternal nature and by existing together with Him would thus deprive Him of His uniqueness.

The problem Aaron now has to face is, as we have seen, the basic problem of the *Kabbalah*. If there is no compositeness in God and if He is the cause of all being, how can the divisions and compositeness evident in His creation be accounted for? The standard Kabbalistic answer is that the *Sephiroth* are the means by which God brought all the worlds into being and it is the *Sephiroth* which are the source of compositeness in creation.[3] Following his master's interpretation of the *Tzimtzum* doctrine, Aaron observes that the *Sephiroth* are called 'instruments' (*kelim*) because they screen the light of *'En Soph* by which all creatures exist. The *Sephiroth* are thus God's instruments in His creative activity, since without such screening there could be no finite world at all. As a result of the Sephirotic process the world appears to be finite. The relationship between *'En Soph* and the *Sephiroth* is described in the Kabbalistic sources on the analogy of the soul in the body. The human soul manifests itself in the body in diverse ways without this affecting the soul's simplicity and non-compositeness. As Aaron has previously stated, and here repeats, the analogy is far from adequate and must not be pressed too closely. For one thing the soul is only non-composite in relation to the body, whereas *'En Soph* is entirely non-composite.

The illustration has only this advantage, that it points to the possibility of a simple entity expressing itself in diverse ways as the soul does in the body. The *Sephirah Ḥesed*, 'Lovingkindness', for example, is the instrument of *'En Soph*. It acts as a screen before the unlimited light of *'En Soph*, so that the latter can function in the limited, particular way of Lovingkindness. Similarly, the *Sephirah Gebhurah*, 'Power', is the instrument by means of which the light of *'En Soph* is confined to express itself in the particular way of Power. So it is with regard to all the

Sephiroth. All variants and changes are not in *'En Soph* but in the instruments which differ from one another, screening and limiting the power of *'En Soph* in diverse ways. These instruments have no independent identity. They are kept in existence by the unchanging, non-composite light of *'En Soph*, extending to them all in equal and unlimited measure. To make this clearer Aaron gives the illustration of the mind of a teacher when he conveys his knowledge to a pupil. The teacher must limit the flow of his wisdom, adapting it to the mental capacity of the pupil. From this point of view it is true that the pupil receives only a limited part of what his teacher has in mind. But for all the self-imposed limitation, the whole of the teacher's mind is 'there'. The limits are not in the teacher's mind itself, but in the revelation of his mind to the pupil.

The *Sephiroth* are called, as has been said, 'instruments' (*kelim*). The instruments used by man serve effectively to fulfil his aims even though they belong to a different order of being from their user and are quite separate from him. Wisdom and the other attributes cannot really be ascribed to God as He is in Himself, because there is no compositeness in Him. This is why Wisdom and the other *Sephiroth* are called 'instruments'. They are of an entirely different order of being from God Himself, but are used by Him. The *Sephiroth* emanate from the divine Nothing. They are also known as 'garments' (*lebhushim*). A man dons different garments for various functions. The garments he wears for casual purposes are different from his more formal wear. But the man inside the clothes is the same. Clothes make the man, but the man does not really suffer any change when he wear's different clothes. God clothes Himself in His *Sephiroth*, but His true essence is simple and suffers no change.

From what has so far been said, it might be concluded that the *Sephiroth* enjoy, in fact, separate being, just as man's instruments and clothes exist apart from the man himself. But the truth is that nothing apart from God, not even the *Sephiroth*, enjoys existence in itself. It is only from *their* point of view, in which the light of *'En Soph* is screened, that the *Sephiroth*, like everything else in creation, have separate being. It is only when speaking figuratively and in a relative sense that we can say that the *Sephiroth* are separate from God.[4] From our point of view the *Sephiroth* appear to enjoy separate existence, like the rays of the sun on earth. But from God's point of view the *Sephiroth* are like the rays of the sun in the sun itself, and they are as naught in His blessed unity. This is the great mystery at the heart of faith. How is it possible for the *Sephiroth* to have the appearance of separate entities and yet be truly one in God? The whole matter, observes Aaron, is beyond all human comprehension.

Here Aaron states his own particular formulation of Ḥabad doctrine. Two terms of which he is particularly fond are: 'from our point of view' (*le-gabê di-dan*) and 'from His point of view' (*le-gabê di-deh*). This is how Aaron seeks to describe the unity of *deus revelatus* and *deus absconditus*. The *Sephiroth* and all creatures enjoy an independent existence from our point of view. But from the point of view of God they are as naught in His unity. Of Moses alone it is said: 'The similitude (*temunah*) of the Lord doth he behold' (Num. 12:8). Aaron's novel interpretation of this verse is that Moses was so lost in God, without a separate identity of his own, that he did not see things as other mortals do, but saw them as God sees them. He beheld them in the 'similitude of God', i.e. he saw that they do not really enjoy separate existence at all. But even Moses' vision was not entirely from God's point of view, for this is impossible to any being apart from God. Moses performed the act of unification, seeing things as they are in reality, united in God. But he, too, beheld only a 'similitude', albeit that he was able to gaze beyond the veil and see only God.

From God's point of view there is no 'similitude' at all. One cannot speak of God seeing only the reality and not the appearance, for this, too, can only be said of humans speaking in human language. From God's point of view the very distinction between appearance and reality is meaningless. Hence Scripture says: 'For ye saw no manner of similitude (*temunah*) on the day that the Lord spoke . . .' (Deut. 4:15). With reference to God's point of view one cannot even speak of a 'similitude' of reality.[5] The Tetragrammaton represents the *Sephiroth*—the first *yod* representing Ḥokhmah, the first *he* Binah, the *waw* the next six *Sephiroth*, and the second *he* Malkhuth, with the point of the *yod* representing Kether. But all this is only from our point of view. In speaking of God's point of view, it is forbidden to make any representation by letters. It is for this reason that in the

Zohar the *Sephiroth* are called 'mysteries' (*sethimin*), *Kether* 'mystery of mysteries' (*sethimo de-sethimin*), while '*En Soph* is called 'mystery above all mysteries' (*sethimo de-khol sethemin*).

Although the *Kabbalah* describes *Kether* as the 'will of '*En Soph*' and there are frequent references to '*En Soph* willing this or that, this must not be taken to mean that one can really speak of a will in '*En Soph*. To will is to suffer change, and '*En Soph* is unchanging. Every reference to this will is intended not as an attempt to describe a process in '*En Soph*, but only as a negation of the view that the world just happened. It is this alone that is meant when it is said that '*En Soph* 'willed' the creation of the world. One cannot even speak of a will 'concealed' in '*En Soph*, for this, too, suggests that it is possible to say something about God as He is in Himself.

When Kabbalists like Cordovero give the illustration of flying sparks when flint is struck to describe the emergence of the *Sephiroth* from '*En Soph*, they do not, in fact, refer to '*En Soph*, but only to the highest point of *Kether*, the point behind *Kether*. This, in the language of the *Kabbalah*, is called 'the hidden mind of *Kether*' (*moḥa sethimo de-kether*).[6]

Here, Aaron goes beyond his sources in extreme negation of any kind of process in '*En Soph*. Every description or attempt at description must never go beyond *Kether*. Of '*En Soph* it is strictly forbidden to say anything at all. In Aaron's own words: 'But from the point of view of '*En Soph* in Himself, as it were, in which there is no comparison whatsoever with any kind of attribute, one cannot even say that attributes are hidden in Him, it cannot be said that the *Sephiroth* become revealed through some action He takes. And this is sufficient for one who understands.'

The problem is not, of course, solved. If there is really no 'will' in '*En Soph*, how can we speak of a 'will' even from our point of view? If nothing can really be said to happen in '*En Soph*, and if, from the point of view of God, there is only simple unity, how does even the appearance of separateness and division among creatures come about? But this again is the question of how the two aspects of the Deity (*deus revelatus* and *deus absconditus*) can be reconciled, and Aaron can only reiterate that the comprehension of this mystery is beyond the reach of the human mind. From the point of view of creatures it is possible to ask: '*Who* created *these*?' No answer will be forthcoming, because at the highest reach of the human mind it is the question alone which can be put. We can only know enough about God to make Him the subject of our question, without pretending that we can ever begin to understand what would be involved in the answer, i.e. in the description of God's nature the answer would entail. But from the point of view of God as He is in Himself even the question is not legitimate.[7]

We have seen that Aaron is careful to hedge round with qualifications any illustration given of the relationship between *'En Soph* and creation. The analogy of the soul in the body is only helpful, for instance, in the following respects. The soul is in itself non-composite (in relation to the body); the soul cannot be known directly, but only through the functions of the body; the soul extends in equal measure to every part of the body to animate the body; and the varied functions of the body do not cause the soul to suffer change. In the same way, *'En Soph* is non-composite; *'En Soph* can only be known through the *Sephiroth*; the light of *'En Soph* extends in equal measure to all creatures to sustain them; and *'En Soph* is unaffected by the differences among the *Sephiroth*.

But in the following respects the analogy breaks down and is completely inadequate: (1) The soul is affected by the body; it experiences bodily functions and changes. (2) Body and soul are two distinct entities. But it is totally incorrect to speak of *'En Soph* being affected by the *Sephiroth* or the worlds beneath them. Furthermore, *'En Soph* must not really be thought of as 'filling' the worlds, for the universe is not a separate entity in which *'En Soph* dwells, since from the point of view of ultimate reality there is only *'En Soph*.[8] 'With regard to the soul being drawn down into the body and her attachment thereto, the soul extends to the bodily organs once these have come into being. If there were no bodily organs, the soul would have nowhere in which it could have expansion. But with regard to the Holy One, Blessed be He, as it were, there is nothing which preceded Him in which He could expand, since there is none else and nothing beside Him, Blessed be He, that one should be able to say that, because He desired something, He extends to it.' There is neither increase nor change in God between the stage before He became 'extended' in creatures and after this has happened. 'The human mind has no power to comprehend this matter clearly. How is it possible for a thing and its contradiction to exist simultaneously? How is it possible for finite and varied worlds of many different kinds, with a special idea inherent in each of their details, yet to be united to the uttermost limits of simplicity, without any other power apart from God, without any change, separation or being whatever, but only God Himself after creation as He was before creation?' We can only conclude that since God is utterly beyond every category of human knowledge and reason, this idea cannot be comprehended at all by the human mind. It follows from all this that the use of the term 'the light of *'En Soph'*, which sustains all creatures, implying as it does something which derives from *'En Soph*, is only to be understood from the point of view of creatures. From the point of view of *'En Soph* there is no *Tzimtzum* and there are no creatures. There is only *'En Soph*. All the Kabbalistic references to the world of emanation are therefore to be understood only in a figurative sense.[9]

It might be thought from all that has been said that, in the *Ḥabad* view, all the divisions in the finite universe are only an illusion and have no real existence. Aaron observes that some have, in fact, thought that this is the meaning of *Ḥabad* doctrine.[10] But Aaron is at pains to refute this and he refuses to use a word like 'illusion' (*dimyon*). The divisions in creation are real enough from our point of view. From this standpoint, there are actual divisions and all created things enjoy an independent existence. What *Ḥabad* teaches is not that the divisions are unreal, but that, from God's point of view, they are absorbed in the infinite light of *'En Soph*. At one and the same time, all creatures enjoy separate existence in all their divisions and are yet united in the single simple unity of *'En Soph*.

This is a marvel (*pele'*) at which we can only express astonishment, but never hope to understand. 'These stages are brought about by God's power, Blessed be He, for otherwise how do they come to be revealed to us? Each one is seen to be a special force and substance in itself. There is a special intention to be observed in each and every creature. The control of all creatures in their categories, status, form and existence, in general and in particular, is, in essence, in the category of separate things. It is not, as some imagine, that the division into stages only appears as such to us, but that in reality they are not in the category of separate entities at all. This is incorrect, since we perceive with our senses that each category has its own particular essential force, all of which God, Blessed be He, wrought intentionally and all by His power, Blessed be He.'[11]

Tzimtzum is thus seen as a screening of the light of *'En Soph*. This is necessary if creatures are to endure. It is essential if God is to be King over His creatures, i.e. if there are to be creatures at all. This is why, among the *Sephiroth*, this screening is represented, in particular, by *Malkhuth*, the divine Sovereignty.[12] The differences between the four worlds of Emanation, Creation, Formation and Action are due to the progressive screening of the divine light. It is in this sense only that we can speak of *Ten Sephiroth* in each of the four worlds. But the light which breaks through the screen to become revealed is the same in all worlds. There are *Ten Sephiroth*, not forty, but in the higher worlds these appear with greater power and less screening than in the lower.[13] The whole purpose of creation is for the veil to be pierced even in this, the lowest world of all. When man engages in divine worship in a spirit of self-sacrifice he cancels out the 'somethingness' of things. By annihilating the self—*bittul ha-yesh*—he thus sees only the divine unity, so that all separateness is dissolved. By means of the divine precepts which man carries out, the divine Will is done on earth. The infinite is then revealed, even in the finite world, and the screen between God and His creation is removed, so that there is only God.

'The whole and chief purpose is for the glory of God to be revealed, even in the external world as it is from our point of view . . . that there should be no divisions even from our point of view. This is brought about by means of our worship and *Torah* study and prayer. For, when the unification of God is affirmed with self-sacrifice, so that the "somethingness" of things is annihilated in its source, all veils and curtains are then broken through and rent asunder, even from our point of view. That is to say, by means of our prayers the unity of God is revealed even in the lower worlds, namely, the lower worlds become annihilated in relation to God's essence, Blessed be He, so that all the worlds are seen no longer in separation and as "something", God forfend. And by means of the *Torah* and the precepts the will of God, Blessed be He, is revealed even in the category of the finite.'[14]

Aaron staunchly defends the view that there is no world at all from God's point of view.[15] He says that 'those lacking in knowledge' are of the opinion that all that is required of the Jew is for him to believe in the incorporeality of God, but the worlds God has created are composed of matter as they seem to us to be. Such Jews believe that God really brought material worlds into being. But such a view can only be defended by accepting one of two propositions, both of which are heretical: (1) Since God is non-corporeal and the worlds are material these worlds must enjoy an existence apart from God. This is the dualistic heresy. (2) God is in the worlds He has created and therefore suffers change as they do. This avoids dualism, but is equally heretical in ascribing change to God.

For Aaron, the only way out of the dilemma is to take the radical step of denying that there are, in reality, any material worlds. From God's point of view there is only God. 'Consequently, we are obliged to believe that the worlds have no existence apart from God, Blessed be He, and that He, Blessed be He, and the worlds are one, for there is nothing apart from Him and nothing outside of Him. They all function solely by His power and in all the worlds is His power alone. . . . It follows that, when it is said that God is incorporeal, this means even from the aspect of the worlds and that all change is only from our point of view and in relation to created things. They are called "worlds" from our point of view, but from God's point of view there is no world at all, for before God, Blessed be He, there is neither *Tzimtzum* nor concealment.' How this is possible is beyond our comprehension, and it is with regard to this mystery that the Rabbis warn us not to engage in speculation on the 'secret things'.

From all the above it is now possible to state the basic thesis upon which Aaron builds his system. The three basic propositions are: (1) *'En Soph* is utterly beyond all human comprehension. (2) There is no world at all from the point of view of God. It is only from our point of view that finite creatures enjoy existence. (3) Just as *'En Soph* is beyond all human comprehension, it is impossible for humans to understand how there can be a world at all, even in appearance, if there is no world from God's point of view. Aaron returns again and again to these themes. With regard to (1) and (3) contemplation is futile. But it is of the greatest significance and value with regard to (2). For only as a result of intense contemplation on this truth can man's heart leap upwards to pierce the veil and behold only God and worship Him in love and fear. We turn now to further consideration by Aaron of these matters.

When we speak of God's self-revelation we use terms like 'God's light'. God emerges, as it were, from the darkness in which He cannot be known into the light in which He can. But all this is only from our point of view. There can be no revelation from His point of view, since the very idea of revelation implies the existence of others, the recipients of revelation and its instruments. However, from God's point of view, there are no others. God's 'light', i.e. His self-revelation, is consequently compared to a garment He puts on: 'He covereth Himself with light as with a garment' (Ps. 104:2). But, like every other analogy used to describe the relationship between God and the world, this is inexact and must not be pressed too far. A garment and the one who wears it are two distinct entities, but God and His light are one. If this is so, how can the light exist at all, how can there be a revelation if, from the point of view of God, the very idea is inadmissible? Aaron can only repeat that this is the great mystery at the heart of faith.[16]

From God's point of view, one cannot even speak of unification, for this term, too, implies the existence of others. Two distinct entities can be unified, but from God's point of view there are no other entities. It is only in the world of division as we see it that one can speak of unification, i.e. we can strive to see everything as united in the simple unity of God. The mystery remains here, too. If there is no meaning to unification from God's point of view, whence comes the need for it in the world of division? How are the divisions we witness possible? One can only conclude that the mystery is beyond the reach of the finite human mind.[17]

Here we arrive at a problem basic to Aaron's system. We have seen that Aaron is extremely reluctant to deny the reality of the Sephirotic worlds and the *Tzimtzum* process. He argues that the *Sephiroth* really do exist and that *Tzimtzum* actually takes place. It is very easy to be misled here, as Aaron acknowledges. He can be misinterpreted as teaching that from God's point of view there are no *Sephiroth* and no *Tzimtzum* at all. But if this were so, there could be neither *Sephiroth* nor *Tzimtzum* from our point of view either. The truth is that God's purpose is revealed in every detail of creation and these really exist. The marvel, beyond all our comprehension, is that from His point of view there are no divisions. It is God's simple, non-composite power, His unique simplicity, which is revealed in unity. Thus, when Aaron states that from God's point of view there is no 'light' of revelation, this should not be taken to mean that there really is no light, but that the light only appears in separateness from Him from our point of view. From God's point of view the 'light' and His essence (i.e. God as He is in Himself and God in the process of self-revelation) are one. It is this which constitutes the marvel, this which is beyond all comprehension. Thus, although we have described Aaron's doctrine to mean that from God's point of view there are no *Sephiroth* and no *Tzimtzum* (and Aaron himself frequently speaks in this vein), in fact, a considerable degree of qualification is here required.

Perhaps what Aaron is trying to say is that we must not think of God creating an 'illusion', but rather of His creating a 'reality', but one which from His point of view enjoys no separateness but is part of His unity. To follow the illustration of the rays of the sun, the rays really do exist even in the sun itself, and they are not an illusion, but in the sun the rays are part of the greater whole and do not there enjoy the separate existence they do on earth. This is a most difficult, if not entirely meaningless, distinction. Aaron's need to make it is clearly psychological. He is concerned to accept the divisions of the material world as real. For, if the details of the material world are illusionary, one cannot adduce them as evidence for the wisdom of the Creator or as a means of apprehending Him. Furthermore, the distinctions between the good and the evil, the sacred and the secular, the holy and the profane would be obliterated.

In Aaron's own words:[18] 'Now although we have explained that all the attributes we use of God, as well as the idea of unification in the world of emanation, are all from our point of view (from the point of view of creatures, which belongs to the category of withdrawal of the light), the reader must not fall into the error of supposing that all the categories of light, *Tzimtzum* and *Sephiroth* are only from our point of view, and that from God's point of view these categories do not obtain at all. For, whoever studies carefully our previous words will notice that, on the contrary, we have explained that even the smallest of the small among the categories has been created with special intention by God, Blessed be He, and that it is God's actual essence which is drawn down into them. What we really mean to suggest is that although God is drawn into the worlds in their category of finiteness, they are not considered as if they were separate entities in relation to God's tremendous exaltedness, Blessed be He, and to His utterly incomprehensible Being so that He is in them without any division whatsoever.'

Aaron refers repeatedly to the great mystery of faith. The whole matter of God's relationship to the world, of how the finite can come out of the Infinite, of how the worlds can exist in their divisions from our point of view and yet to be in simple unity from God's point of view, all this, says Aaron, is 'higher than reason' (*le-maʿalah min ha-sekhel*). Aaron devotes considerable space in his work to a consideration of what is meant by the term 'higher than reason' as applied to the divine mysteries.[19] The medieval philosophers also speak of God as 'higher than reason', but they mean by this that His wisdom is too elevated for humans to grasp. They do not generally deny that God's wisdom is of the same order as our wisdom, but affirm that it is infinitely greater. For them a divine mystery means a subject so profound that the finite human mind cannot comprehend it, but it belongs none the less to comprehension. The categories with which one operates, even in this sphere, are still those of conceptual thought, but a distinction is made between matters for which the human mind is an adequate instrument of comprehension and those too difficult for human conception. There is, in other words, a divine and a human conception.

This, Aaron is at pains to refute. God is utterly *beyond* conception. It is not that His thoughts are *higher* than our thoughts, but that the whole idea of conceptual thought is too inferior to be attributed to Him. The difference is one of kind, not alone of degree. Drawing on an illustration given by Schneor Zalman, Aaron says that one cannot remark of a particularly profound mental concept that it is impossible to touch it physically. A mental concept, by its very nature, cannot be held in the physical hand. The idea of 'higher than reason' as applied to God means that the category of conceptual thought is as little applicable to Him as is the notion of physical grasp to a mental concept.

The Rabbis say, for instance, that the ark in the Holy of Holies did not occupy any space (*B.B.* 99a). Similarly, they say that the words *Zakhor* ('*Remember* the Sabbath day' in Ex. 20:8) and *Shamor* ('*Keep* the Sabbath day' in Deut. 5:12) were pronounced by God in a single utterance 'which the mouth cannot utter and the ear hear' (*Sheb.* 20b). Now, these are quite different from the Biblical miracles, for example, in that they offend against the laws of thought. For water to stand firm like a wall or for an axe to float is a suspension of natural law. To say that an ark is in a given place and yet is not there, or that two words were uttered when one was uttered, is equivalent to saying that A=not-A. Since the medieval thinkers understood the term 'higher than reason' in the above-mentioned sense (that God's thought, too, is conceptual), the commentators among them, like Abraham Ibn Ezra, deny that such things are really possible and treat these Talmudic passages as legendary.[20] God, for them, is also bound by the laws of logic. He can do that which is impossible for us, but He cannot do the absolutely impossible. (They would presumably argue that this does not impose limits on God's power, since the absolutely impossible is meaningless. To say that God cannot make A equal not-A is simply to say that God cannot . . . without completing the sentence.)[21]

But Aaron believes that Ibn Ezra and others who thought like him erred because they were ignorant of the *Kabbalah*. As the *Kabbalah* understands it, God is 'higher than reason' in the sense that He is not bound by the rules of conceptual thinking. From God's point of view, contradictions can exist simultaneously. For God there can be a finite world of divisions and yet be no finite world of divisions.[22] Wisdom (*Hokhmah*) is but an instrument which God uses, but He can fulfil His will without it, just as a man's personality is in no way affected by the absence of an instrument he has once chosen to use.

It is true, observes Aaron, that now that there is a creation, God's wondrous wisdom is seen manifested in it. But the basic problem of how the material universe can possibly be an instrument for the revelation of the spiritual remains a mystery and one that is utterly beyond the very conception of wisdom. Hence the benediction recited after bodily evacuation begins with the words: 'Blessed art Thou, O Lord our God, King of the universe, *who hast formed man in wisdom*', but concludes: 'Blessed art Thou O Lord, who art *the wondrous healer of all flesh*.' For all the evidence of the divine wisdom in creation, there is an element of sheer wonder and marvel (*pele'*) at the heart of things.

Aaron turns[23] to a discussion of the most difficult theological problem of the Middle Ages, how God's foreknowledge can be reconciled with man's freedom of choice. Since God knows before a man is born how he will behave during his lifetime (this is implied in the belief in God's omniscience), all man's deeds must be determined. How, then, can he be free? Various are the solutions offered by the medieval thinkers.[24]

Maimonides[25] does not hesitate to state boldly that the solution to the problem is beyond the grasp of the human mind. To discuss it adequately, man would have to know what is meant by God's 'knowledge', but, since in God His Essence and His knowledge are one and the same, man can as little hope to grasp the mystery as he can hope to comprehend God's nature. On the whole the early Hasidic teachers either avoided the discussion of this problem entirely or were content to refer to it as insoluble. All that was necessary for man, they implied, is for him to accept both horns of the dilemma. Man is free and yet God has foreknowledge.[26] Schneor Zalman is the exception. He tries to deal with the problem on the basis of his distinction between the universe as seen by us and the universe as seen from the point of view of God. Aaron's views are an elaboration of the views of his master, but constitute an advance on them.

Schneor Zalman does not really go far beyond those medieval thinkers who suggested that God's foreknowledge is not determinative, i.e. God does know beforehand that man will behave in a particular way, but this knowledge does not compel man to act in that way. Naturally this does nothing to solve the problem, for this is precisely the problem, how can God's *certain* foreknowledge fail to be determinative? What Schneor Zalman does do is to set forth the 'solution' in terms of his basic views on *Tzimtzum*. God's foreknowledge, he says, belongs to the

Supernal Mind. This 'surrounds' man, but does not enter into his life in the way that the lower *Sephiroth* do. Consequently, man is unmoved by God's foreknowledge and it has no effect on his freedom of choice.[27]

Aaron's thought, never easy, is particularly involved when dealing with this question. If I understand him correctly, he appears to be saying that the problem is caused by a failure to appreciate the distinction between God's point of view and our own. From our point of view there is, indeed, no foreknowledge and man is therefore free. For time is real from our point of view. There is past, present and future. We must not think of God knowing in the past what will happen in the future. This is not legitimate, since from God's point of view past, present and future are one. The real problem is not that of foreknowledge versus free will, but of the very notion of *fore*knowledge. This term only has meaning in the time sequence from our point of view. If it be asked how the idea of foreknowledge can exist if there is no foreknowledge from God's point of view, this is simply a restatement of the basic problem of how there can be a finite world at all. With this wider question Aaron's work is concerned, the question of how the abyss between God's point of view and ours can be spanned.

In the final analysis one must fall back here, as Aaron does, on the idea of the marvel (*pele'*) of which he speaks so frequently. The novelty in Aaron's thought is that he sees the problem of foreknowledge versus free will in terms of the wider problem of the very existence of a finite world. This latter problem is, indeed, an insoluble mystery; it is, as Aaron has said, 'higher than reason'. But, once this mystery has been accepted as an act of faith, there is no further problem of foreknowledge versus free will, for in speaking of foreknowledge we are using a term which really belongs in the category of God's point of view, whereas in speaking of free will we are speaking from our point of view. It might be helpful to formulate all this in Aaron's own terminology.

Aaron begins[28] by referring to Maimonides' formulation of the problem and to the fact that all the great thinkers, Kabbalists and philosophers, have grappled with it. His statement of the problem is as follows: 'If the Holy One, Blessed be He, knows all the deeds of the sons of men before creation, then they are compelled to behave in the way they do, whether for good or ill, by virtue of His knowledge, Blessed be He. How then can there be free will and punishment?' Aaron observes in reply that the Rabbis never speak of God *knowing* beforehand what man will do, but of God *seeing* all the deeds of man. From God's point of view, 'before' creation one cannot speak of 'knowledge' at all. At that stage, as it were, all divisions, including those which follow on man's freedom of choice and including the very distinction between good and evil, are in the category of one simple force. It is only from the point of view of creation, as a result of *Tzimtzum*, that the detailed divisions actually enjoy existence.[29] All the divisions exist, as it were, in potentiality, from the beginning, but it is through man's freedom of choice that they are actualized, that they become revealed.

For instance, the Rabbis might say that a certain man was destined to become what he eventually became. This should not be understood in a fatalistic way, that God decreed that he should so become, but that his 'potential' career was 'there' right from the beginning. This potential was there to be realized, but only through man's own efforts. The potential force cannot but be realized, but if man does not make the necessary effort it would find its realization in some other way, e.g. by means of metempsychosis.[30] Aaron has hardly succeeded in removing the difficulties. His chief concern in this passage is to reject a fatalistic doctrine. Man is entirely free to realize or not his potential force which cries out for realization. But in one way or another, sooner or later, the force will be realized.

An important summary of Aaron's views is to be found in his lengthy note in the fourth part of his *Sha'are Ha-Yihud We-Ha-'Emunah*.[31] The *Midrash*[32] states that four Biblical characters expressed differing ideas on God in His relationship to the world. Jethro said: 'Now I know that the Lord is greater than all gods' (Ex. 18:11). Jethro was not a true monotheist, but a henotheist. He acknowledged the existence of other gods, but believed that God was greater than they. In the words of the *Midrash*, he 'attributed reality to idols'. Naaman said: 'Behold now, I know that there is no God in all the earth, but in Israel' (II Kings 5:15). He recognized that there are no other gods upon earth. Rahab said: 'For the Lord your God, He is God in heaven above, and on earth beneath' (Josh. 2:11). She acknowledged the one God in both heaven and earth, but, in the words of the *Midrash*, 'left Him out of the space of the world', i.e. she thought of God as filling heaven and earth, but not the space between them. But Moses said: 'The Lord, He is God in heaven above and upon the earth beneath; there is none else' (Deut. 4:39). 'There is none else' means 'even in the space of the world'. Aaron, allowing himself considerable licence, understands the *Midrash* as expressing four different views regarding the relationship between God and His creation.

According to Aaron's interpretation, there are four stages in comprehension of the nature of the finite world in its relation to God.

(1) *The stage of Jethro*

Jethro did not really believe in the existence of other gods. His error was that he attributed reality of an ultimate kind to 'that which is' (*yesh*). The term 'the Lord' (=the Tetragrammaton) represents the inner power of God. The term 'other gods' represents the external control and management of the world by means of the 'seventy princes', i.e. the powers God brings into being as a result of the *Tzimtzum* process. Jethro believed that 'the Lord' is greater than these 'other gods', that is to say, he acknowledged they are utterly dependent on God, but they do exist, they are real. On this view, real worlds came into being as a result of *Tzimtzum*, albeit these are completely dependent on God. The idea of unification on this view means that man acknowledges that the external management of the worlds is really 'annihilated' in the inner power and control of God's simple unity. The worlds exist in their own right and not for some other purpose. It was God's intention that they should enjoy real existence.

(2) *The stage of Naaman*

Naaman went further than Jethro. In his view the whole purpose of *Tzimtzum* and the emergence of the worlds was not for the worlds to enjoy an existence in their own right, but solely in order that the glory of God be revealed upon earth through the deeds of Israel. But Naaman did not believe that the manifestation of God's glory upon earth was His sole purpose in creation. In the finite world this was, indeed, God's purpose, but in the

'EN SOPH AND THE UNIVERSE

realms of the Infinite there could be no thought of God's particular manifestation in the finite. A great king, for example, might build splendid edifices whereby to impress the inhabitants of a tiny village. So far as the villagers are concerned, the erection of the buildings is the king's sole purpose, but they do not imagine that the king has no other interest than to impress these poor folk with his majesty. They are fully aware that the king has many and varied interests far beyond the narrow confines of their limited horizons. Therefore, Naaman said: 'There is no God *in all the earth*, but in Israel', i.e. so far as this earth is concerned, the purpose of creation is for Israel to make manifest God's glory. But the heavenly realms are so far above all finite creatures that it is absurd to see in them, too, the fulfilment of God's purposes in terms of His manifestation in and through Israel.

(3) *The stage of Rahab*

Rahab saw more deeply into the truth. She acknowledged that even in heaven the sole purpose is for God's glory to be revealed in the finite. She saw that from God's point of view, in His infinite power, there is no difference between the hidden worlds and the revealed ones. Her error was that, while recognizing that there is only God's simple unity from God's point of view, she thought that from the point of view of God's revelation in the worlds there is an infinite gulf between the divisions of the finite world and the simple unity of *'En Soph*. This is expressed by the saying that Rahab left God out of the space of the world, i.e. she believed in an infinite space or division between God as He is in Himself and God as manifested in the world, not, indeed, from God's point of view, but from the point of view of creatures.

(4) *The stage of Moses*

Moses saw that there is only God, that even though the worlds appear to be real, they are truly only the manifestations of the light of *'En Soph*. The worlds only have the appearance of an independent existence from our point of view, but from God's point of view there is nothing else even after *Tzimtzum*. Thus, Moses said: 'The Lord (=the Tetragrammaton=God's simple unity), He is God (=*Tzimtzum*) in heaven above and in the earth beneath (=there is, from His point of view, no difference between the two aspects at all and, therefore,): there is none else.'

In Aaron's own words: 'Rahab did acknowledge that from the point of view of God's essence He is the same in all things, in heaven and in earth. But it was necessary for God's revelation, Blessed be He, to emerge from the category of "heaven" to that of "earth". From the point of view of God's revelation, this produces a "space", that is to say, a "concealment". For without such a "concealment" there could have been no revelation in the category of "earth" at all. Consequently, it was necessary for *Tzimtzum* to be in the category of revelation.

'Now, Rahab imagined that *Tzimtzum* was in the nature of a substance apart from God's substance, as it were. For all the difference between the two, she compared the process to that of a man who is moved to concentrate on some very lowly thing. In the category of the "hidden" this is because that lowly thing touches his very being. But in the category of the "revealed" he is obliged to limit his being so as to clothe his wisdom in aspects quite separate from his being, etc. It follows that this "clothing" constitutes an addition to him and separate from his essence, etc. So Rahab imagined it was with regard to God's revelation in the worlds. She did not, therefore, say "there is none else", for, as she saw it, the worlds are something else, that is to say, something apart from the revelation of God's essence. And this is sufficient for one who understands. But, in reality, there is nothing else, even from the point of view of God's revelation. It is only from our point of view that it appears as something separate from God. And the main purpose was that there should be nothing else from the aspect of revelation. And this is brought about by Israel's worship.'

By these last remarks Aaron means that Israel, even in this finite world, can, by their unification of God and by their self-sacrifice, 'annihilate' all the worlds which appear as 'something' (*yesh*) apart from God and, in this way, they affirm that there is nothing apart from God, even here on earth. Thus, the *Zohar* speaks of the power of prayer and *Torah* study to break through the heavenly divisions. This refers to the whole *Tzimtzum* process by means of which the division comes about between God as *'En Soph* and His revelation after *Tzimtzum*. But from God's point of view, there is no difference, and even from man's point of view the division is broken down by means of prayer and study in a spirit of self-sacrifice. However, the removal of the barriers can never be complete in this world. By bestirring himself in holiness man, in this life, can, at best, break through the divisions. In this world the 'somethingness' of things is bound to act as a barrier, because the spiritual atmosphere is impure. Furthermore, not all men have the same capacity for piercing the veils. Some attain to a revelation of the divine in the temples of the World of Action, others the higher stage of revelation in the temples of the World of Formation, and others, higher still, of the World of Creation. But no human being can attain to the revelation of the divine in the category of the temples of the World of Emanation, for, at this stage, there is, as yet, no division at all.

All this applies to this world. But in the Messianic Age, when the spirit of impurity will be banished from earth, God will be revealed even in the finite world, without any concealment whatsoever. Aaron concludes: 'Consequently, all our worship at the present time is to purify the atmosphere by means of *Torah* study, the practice of the precepts, and prayer. By means of our worship we remove the *Tzimtzum* which comes from concealment, but not in actuality, for it remains in the category of concealment. In the future, however, the revelation will be complete even in the "somethingness", as a result of Israel's worship in this world through their annihilation to the category of revelation in the category of the worlds. Then the divine will be revealed in the category of uniformity, as it is said: "They shall see eye to eye" (Is. 52:8). And this is sufficient for one who understands. Understand it well.'

Aaron, as we have seen, repeatedly refers to the 'marvel' (*pele'*). This consists of the strange concept that, while from God's point of view there is only one simple power, yet all the worlds exist in their divisions. This is brought about by the divine will, which is 'higher than reason' and hence must be incomprehensible to humans. Aaron adds, however, that even to speaks of this as a 'marvel' is only permissible from our point of view. We do see the worlds in their separateness, and because we cannot comprehend how this can be, we say it is wondrous and marvellous. But from God's point of view there are no worlds at all and one cannot therefore speak, from His point of view, of their existence as a 'marvel'.[33] Another aspect of the 'marvel' (*pele'*) must also be noted. There is undoubtedly an increase of divine light by means of the worship of God by finite creatures who fulfil His will. Does this mean that there is change in Him? Again the solution to the difficulty is to be found in the familiar distinction between God's point of view and our own. But again how is this possible? And once again the principle of the 'marvel' must be invoked.[34]

Aaron concludes his first volume with the words: 'All the worlds were created only for man that he might attach them to God, Blessed be He, in unity by means of his worship. Without the category of unification through man's worship one cannot attribute to God, Blessed be He, any worlds at all nor any other category at all, as the student will understand from the words which have been recorded in these gates.'

NOTES TO CHAPTER SIX

[1] *SYE*, Introduction, p. 4a.

[2] *SYE*, *Shaʿar* I, Chap. 1, pp. 5a–6a. These comments and the next two paragraphs are based on this passage.

[3] *SYE*, *ibid.*, Chap. 2, pp. 6b–9a. The text down to 'have separate being' on p. 92 is based on this passage.

[4] *SYE*, *ibid.*, Chap. 3, pp. 9a–10a. These comments and the next two paragraphs are based on this passage.

[5] *SYE*, *ibid.*, pp. 9a–10a. The idea of Moses seeing things from God's point of view is found, too, in the writings of Yitzhak Isaac Epstein of Homel, which shows that the idea probably goes back to Schneor Zalman himself, v. Bunim, *op. cit.*, *Mishneh Ḥabad, Mishnath Ha-Nebhuah*, Chap. 3, p. 17, who quotes from *Ḥanah 'Ariel* of Epstein to Num., p. 341, and pp. 48–b.

[6] *SYE*, *ibid.*, Chap. 4, pp. 11a–12a. The text down to 'beyond the reach of the human mind' on p. 94 is based on this passage.

[7] *SYE*, *ibid.*, Chap. 5, p. 12b.

[8] *SYE*, *ibid.*, Chap. 25, pp. 48a–50a. The text down to 'cannot be comprehended at all by the human mind' on p. 96 is based on this passage.

[9] *SYE*, *ibid.*, Chap. 26, p. 51a.

[10] *SYE*, *Shaʿar* II, Chap. 8, p. 10b.

[11] *SYE*, *ibid.*, p. 10b.

[12] *SYE*, *ibid.*, Chap. 12, p. 16b.

[13] *SYE*, *ibid.*, Chap. 13, p. 17a.

[14] *SYE*, *ibid.*, Chap. 15, pp. 21a–b.

[15] *SYE*, *ibid.*, Chap. 26, pp. 37a–b.

[16] *SYE*, *ibid.*, Chap. 27, p. 38a.

[17] *SYE*, *ibid.*, pp. 39a–b.

[18] *SYE*, *ibid.*, Chap. 28, p. 40a.

NOTES

[19] *SYE, Shaʿar* III, Chap. 14, p. 15a.

[20] *V.* Ibn Ezra: Commentary to Ex. 20:1.

[21] *V.* Antony Flew: 'Divine Omnipotence and Human Freedom' in *New Essays in Philosophical Theology*, SCM Press, 1955, pp. 144 f.

[22] *SYE, ibid.*, Chap. 14, pp. 15a–16a. These comments and the next paragraph refer to this passage.

[23] *SYE, ibid.*, Chap. 38, pp. 46a–52b.

[24] *V.* Isaac Husik: *A History of Mediaeval Jewish Philosophy*, Jewish Publication Society of America, Philadelphia, 1940, Index: 'Freedom of the Will'.

[25] *V. Yad, Hil. Teshubhah*, V.5.

[26] *V.* Teitelbaum, *op. cit.*, Part II, Chap. 5, pp. 121–6.

[27] *V. Liqqute Torah*, Numbers, Zhitomer, 1866, Ba-Midbar, s.v. mi gilah, cf. Teitelbaum, *op. cit.*, pp. 123–6, Bunim, *op. cit.*, Mishneh Ḥabad, Mishnath Ha-Nephesh, Chap. 6, pp. 71–72.

[28] *SYE, ibid.*, Chap. 38, pp. 46a–b.

[29] *SYE, ibid.*, pp. 48a–49b.

[30] *SYE, ibid.*, pp. 51a–52a, *v.* the lengthy note on the theme of fatalism, pp. 35a–52b.

[31] *SYE, Shaʿar* IV, note on pp. 22b–44b, particularly pp. 39a–44b. The text down to 'Understand it well' on p. 109 is based on this passage.

[32] Deut. R. 2:27, *Yalqut*, 269.

[33] *SYE, Shaʿar* V, Chap. 23, p. 28a.

[34] *SYE, ibid.*, Chap. 25, p. 29a.

CHAPTER SEVEN

Man's Worship

'Know this day, and lay it to thy heart, that the Lord, He is God in heaven above and upon the earth beneath; there is none else' (Deut. 4:39). This verse contains, for Aaron, the three basic elements in man's worship of God. '*Know* this day' refers to contemplation on the theme that 'there is none else', that all is in God. We have seen in our consideration of Aaron's earlier work the significance of contemplation in Aaron's scheme and in *Ḥabad* generally. Secondly, the emotions must be involved. As a result of deep contemplation on the theme that all is in God, man's heart is moved to love and fear Him. Hence the verse goes on to say: 'And lay it to thy *heart*.'

But, as we have seen, for *Ḥabad* the highest form of divine worship is to carry out God's will in practice. The deed is particularly significant since, by means of concrete action in the physical world, man elevates the lowest stage of creation to link it with its source in God. This aspect of worship is referred to in the words 'and upon the *earth* beneath'. By *acting* in accordance with God's will, man demonstrates that His sovereignty is not confined to the heavenly realms. These three—thought, feeling and action—follow one from the other. First, there must be contemplation of the divine. This generates powerful religious emotions which in turn inspire religious acts.[1]

Both the animal soul and the divine soul of man express themselves through thought, feeling and action. For all that, the main expression of the animal soul is through the emotions, whereas the divine soul expresses itself mainly through the mind. It is the divine soul which is particularly effective in helping man to attain to the stage of self-annihilation when he engages in contemplation. Aaron's reading of Ecclesiastes 3:21 is: 'Who knoweth the spirit of man, which goeth upward, and the spirit of the beast, which goeth downward to the earth?' The 'spirit of the beast'—the animal soul—has the effect of compelling man to gaze downwards, that is to say, to see things 'from our point of view', in separateness. But the 'spirit of man'—the divine soul—compels man to gaze upwards to see all things as they are 'from God's point of view', in their simple unity. Since by nature man sees things in their separateness, he can only awaken the powers of the divine soul by engaging in contemplation. Through profound reflection on the tremendous idea that there are no divisions in reality and that all is in God, man's divine soul is helped to exert its influence on the emotions, so that he is moved in self-annihilation.

We have seen that *da'ath* (the third word in the *Ḥabad* trilogy) means involvement with whatever idea one contemplates. It is that aspect of man's psychological attitude which prevents contemplation from being irrelevant to his life in its wholeness. It is by means of *da'ath* that the thing contemplated has an effect on the emotions, and these in turn an effect on action. *Da'ath* can thus be said to have a purifying effect. Without it, man's emotions would be entirely self-centred, with his intellect engaged in no more than a purely academic way. *Da'ath* is the name given to man's effort to transform contemplation from an academic exercise into religious engagement. In the language of present-day Existentialism, *da'ath* is commitment.

This takes us to the heart of the problem involved in contemplation. There is a great paradox here. On the one hand, unless the heart is moved as a result of contemplation, the latter has no effect of any significance. But, on the other hand, it is impossible for man to have any powerful emotional experience, without becoming aware of himself through the sensation he feels. Consequently, all contemplation leading to ecstasy can only be vindicated when *da'ath* has done its work. Through *da'ath*, man senses the true sweetness of self-annihilation in God. This very experience enables him to see how false and vain is self-awareness, so that there is constant tension in the contemplative life between self-awareness and self-abnegation in God.

The divine soul is only able to function through the processes of the animal soul. It is consequently a grave mistake to imagine that there can be a kind of ecstasy of the divine soul alone in its purity. The relationship between the two souls can be compared to that of silver and the soil in which it is found. It is quite impossible to extract pure silver directly from the earth. At first, silver and soil are so intermingled that they can only be separated by a repeated series of refinements in a crucible. The divine soul's silver is similarly intermingled with the animal soul's dross. It follows that if, for example, a man does not eat and so weakens his mental capacity, this will prevent the divine soul from obtaining to nearness of God, since the divine soul depends on the animal soul. Prayer is the crucible in which the silver of the divine soul is refined.

The stages in the act of contemplation are, first, a powerful sensation experienced in the animal soul as a result of contemplation (i.e. a purely natural response to the 'thrill' of reflection on the divine), and then the refinement of this sensation so that the self enjoys the experience, and yet without self-awareness. It is the self which experiences God. Without sensation in the heart there is no experience of God, only abstract thought about Him. This latter can hardly be referred to as 'Wisdom' (*Hokhmah*) or 'Understanding' (*Binah*). But the very nature of a true experience of God involves self-annihilation. The whole process is bound to be exceedingly subtle. It is vital for the self to be deeply affected; yet once the self has attained to a realization that God is all, the self must pale into insignificance. There cannot be an authentic self-annihilation unless there is a self to be annihilated. The silver of self-annihilation is, at first, inseparable from the dross of self.

This whole question loomed very large in *Habad* thought and practice. Naturally, a contemplative movement not infrequently found the role of the emotions in the religious life somewhat embarrassing. We have evidence from the writings of Rabbi Dobh Baer, of Lübavitch son and successor of Schneor Zalman and Aaron's great rival, that many *Hasidim*, after the death of the *Habad* founder, were extremely puzzled as to the attitude *Habad* adopts towards ecstasy (*hithpaʻaluth*) in prayer. Some declared that *Habad* forbids every kind of sensed ecstasy as a sensation of 'that which is' (*yesh*), forbidden to those who wished to gaze beyond the 'somethingness' of things to see only God. Others, again, taught that the whole aim of contemplation is to induce ecstasy.

It was to deal with this question that Dobh Baer wrote his famous 'Tract on Ecstasy' (*Qunteros Ha-Hithpaʻaluth*).[2] Like Aaron, Dobh Baer argues that ecstasy is important, indeed essential, for unless it comes there is only abstract, academic thought and no experience of the divine. There is only thought about God and no meeting with or experience of God. But Dobh Baer appears to be far more strict than Aaron in distinguishing between authentic and unauthentic ecstasy. Dobh Baer's 'Tract on Ecstasy' is, in the main, an acute analysis of the different forms ecstasy can assume, in an attempt to distinguish the real from the sham. Aaron shows a similar concern, but he does not entirely reject even the sham type of ecstasy. One can state the difference between Dobh Baer and Aaron (which, in addition to other considerations, as we have seen, led to the setting up of two rival Ḥabad schools) in this way. For Dobh Baer, ecstasy is positively harmful and therefore to be severely discouraged, unless it is of the authentic type. For Aaron, ecstasy, as the only way of extracting the silver from the dross, is so important that he is prepared to encourage it even to the extent of risking spurious ecstasy and not frowning too severely on this latter type. Furthermore, Aaron is not impressed by glib talk about authentic and unauthentic ecstasy. A good deal depends on the person involved, and what is sham for one well advanced on the mystical path may be authentic for one of lesser rank.[3]

Aaron claims that his master, Schneor Zalman, was far from strict in rejecting spurious ecstasy. 'Now although I have written above in the name of our teacher, his soul is in Eden, that man's labour in worship should be to purge himself of self-awareness, nevertheless all his holy words were always to encourage the heart to validate every type of ecstasy according to each person's capacity. No man's heart should be disturbed because of his realization that the ideal type of human worship and ecstasy should be one from which all self-awareness has been removed and in which there is no admixture of evil. For a man may come to view with suspicion all ecstasy, in his fear that it may contain a measure of self-awareness and that his love is illusory, imperfectly refined and unauthentic. The result may be that he will not allow himself to engage in the type of contemplation which extends to love sensed in the heart. Therefore, he (Schneor Zalman) would validate every kind of love, and he urged his followers not to be apprehensive about the illusory nature of the love.

'The whole of his holy work (the *Tanya*) is based on the

verse: "But the word is very nigh unto thee, in thy mouth, and in thy heart, that thou mayest do it" (Deut. 30:14). And the student of his holy work will perceive that all his words are intended for the encouragement of the ecstasy of each one, in whatever fashion it may be, and not, God forfend, to reject it.

'My teacher, his soul is in Eden, further expounded the verse: "My dove, my undefiled" (Cant. 6:9). He interpreted the word *yonah* ("dove") as if it were an expression denoting "fraud" (*'ona'ah*). No one, said he, need be apprehensive that his worship is fraudulent, containing an admixture of good and evil, for even if it is fraudulent it is still undefiled. Even though it is necessary for man to refine his sensations, yet here self-knowledge is essential. It is necessary for each one to know himself and to assess his capacity for ridding himself of this admixture. All this is involved in worship, and the battle is joined at the hour of prayer. But in battle sometimes one side is victorious, sometimes the other. Should one, on this account, not engage in battle at all? If this were so, the enemy would prevail utterly, and man would remain entirely in the hands of the "Other Side", his animal soul.

'It should be remembered, too, that this victory is in accordance with each one's capacity, and that there is an infinite number of stages. What would be considered for one worshipper an absence of self-awareness would be for another worshipper, of higher degree, self-awareness. For there is an infinite number of stages, so that the annihilation of this sensation in one of humble degree is considered as self-awareness for one of more elevated degree. It is with reference to a matter such as this that the Rabbis say: "It is not thy duty to complete the work, but neither art thou free to desist from it." This means that man is obliged to deal hardly with himself in worship, with the labour of soul and flesh, in order to uncover the hidden love of the heart by means of knowledge and understanding. But it is not his duty to complete the work by attaining perfection; each person should strive to the best of his ability.'

The three aspects of worship—contemplation, emotional ecstasy and practice of the precepts—are all necessary. Man's worship is incomplete if any one of them is missing. Contemplation is necessary, for it is only by the use of the intellect that the emotions can be purified and be authentic in their yearning for

God. Emotion in ecstasy is necessary as the test of whether contemplation is truly profound or nothing more than an irrelevant intellectual exercise. Practice is most important of all, for God's will is truly expressed in the practical precepts and in this way is linked to the world of 'somethingness' (*yesh*). Through the performance of the good deed in the world of 'somethingness'— through the use of the material world in the service of God—this 'somethingness' becomes annihilated in God. In other words, this is the highest degree of worship precisely because it utilizes the material world, which is the most remote of all worlds from God, and brings even this to God. Practice even on its own, without either contemplation or ecstasy, is still of some value, for, after all, God's will has been done.

Similarly, ecstasy, even without contemplation, unauthentic though it must be, is still of value in helping man to turn from evil and do good. But contemplation on its own is valueless, since, by definition, really profound contemplation must result in ecstasy. It is not so much that contemplation without ecstasy is valueless as that without ecstasy it is not contemplation. Unless there is sensation in the heart, contemplation is *about* God, but is in no way an experience of Him.

Aaron concludes his Introduction to his second volume (*Sha'are 'Abhodah*) by reminding his readers that this volume is based on the first part of Schneor Zalman's *Liqqute 'Amarim* (i.e. the first section of the *Tanya*). Since this deals with the worship of what Schneor Zalman calls: 'average men' (*benonim*), Aaron's sub-title is *'Abhodath Ha-Benonim* ('Average Men's Worship').

It should be noted that this term *benoni* ('average man') has a special technical meaning in Ḥabad. For Ḥabad,[4] the *Tzaddiq*, the 'righteous man', is the saint who has slain every desire for evil in himself and desires God alone. The *Rasha'*, the 'wicked man', is the man in complete bondage to the evil within him. The *Benoni* is not, as conventionally understood, one whose sins and virtues are equally balanced. Rather is he one who never sins consciously, but, unlike the *Tzaddiq*, there is within him a constant war between the good and the evil. The *Benoni*, then, is a person far advanced on the road to perfection, but not yet to the stage of the *Tzaddiq*. Consequently, the whole purpose of the book is to describe in detail the stages of worship for this type of 'average man'. Not all matters in the book are for the uninitiated, remarks Aaron, but all can benefit from parts of it at least.

According to the *Kabbalah*, the main purpose of man's worship is to unite the Holy One, Blessed be He, with His *Shekhinah*. Man on this finite earth, in which there is the indwelling Presence of God, brings about this unification by reaching out to God in worship and thus elevating the world he inhabits. We have noted above how in Zoharic *Kabbalah* the Holy One, Blessed be He, denotes the *Sephirah* of *Tiphereth*, whereas the *Shekhinah* denotes *Malkhuth*. In the Lurianic *Kabbalah* the idea of this unification is broadened so that the Holy One, Blessed be He, represents God in His aspect of concealment, whereas the *Shekninah* represents God in His aspect of revelation. Aaron follows the *Ḥabad* scheme in interpreting the idea of this unification in even broader terms. To say this is not, however, to imply that Aaron is conscious of any fresh developments in his thought. He appears to have been convinced that the *Ḥabad* interpretation is actually that of the earlier *Kabbalah*. Nor, for that matter, would he ever have accepted the view that the Lurianic concept differs from the original Zoharic concept.

What, for Aaron, do the terms 'the Holy One, Blessed be He' and 'the *Shekhinah*' denote? The first term, he says,[5] refers to all the different powers, stages, forces, divisions as they are from God's point of view. They are then in the potential stage. Although potentially they are different, yet by virtue of the 'marvel' (*pele'*), of which Aaron speaks so frequently, they are in reality one simple, undivided force. This is impossible for humans. There cannot be division and unity at one and the same time. But nothing is impossible for God. The term 'the Holy One, Blessed be He' refers, then, to the divisions of all worlds in potentiality, as they are from God's point of view. In the *Kabbalah*, says Aaron, this aspect of Deity is also called *Zeʻer Anpin* ('Lesser Countenance' or 'Short Suffering') as opposed to *'Arikh 'Anpin* ('Long Countenance' or 'Long Suffering'), i.e. God as He is in Himself in the aspect of *Kether*, the highest of the *Sephiroth*. This aspect of 'the Holy One, Blessed be He' is also represented by the Tetragrammaton which, according to its root meaning, signifies Being in Itself. The united forces as they are in God are also called 'The Higher Unification'.

The term *Shekhinah*, on the other hand, refers to God's indwelling Presence in the worlds after they have emerged from potentiality to actuality. Here, the divisions are seen as separate from God, yet even here there is only God. This aspect is also known as *Malkhuth*, 'Sovereignty' because, at this stage, God has become King over His creatures revealed in all their separateness and divisions. This aspect is also known as 'the Female' (*Nuqbhah*), the passive principle, as opposed to *Ze'er* (*'Anpin*) the male, active principle. This aspect of the *Shekhinah* is God's creative activity as seen from our point of view. For man to recognize, even from his point of view, that all is unity is to perform the 'Lower Unification'.

Aaron[6] sees this in the verse: 'I am the Lord, that is My name; And My glory will I not give to another' (Is. 42:8). 'I am the Lord' (=the Tetragrammaton) refers to 'the Holy One, Blessed be He', to creation from God's point of view. The 'name' of a person is that by virtue of which he is known. Hence the words 'that is My name' refer to the *Shekhinah*, God as revealed in creation, the process as it appears from our point of view. But both aspects are really one. The aspect of God's revelatory activity is due to *Tzimtzum*, but, in reality, even that which is seen from our point of view is God's simple unity. The verse consequently states: 'I am the Lord, *that* is My name.' There is, in reality, nothing apart from God. Even His 'glory' (=God as revealed to His creatures) is not given to another.

One way of looking at all this is to see that which is revealed (that which is seen from our point of view) as 'lower' than that which is seen from God's point of view. But the very existence of the finite world belongs to the great 'marvel' (*pele'*) of explaining any existence apart from God. This marvel reaches back to God's essence, and utterly beyond human comprehension. The 'lower' the degree the greater the 'marvel' and hence the nearer, paradoxically enough, to God. It can, therefore, be said that God's Sovereignty (*Malkhuth*) has its 'root' in God as He is in Himself. According to this way of looking at the matter, the 'root' of the *Shekhinah* is 'higher' than that of 'the Holy One, Blessed be He'. This, says Aaron,[7] is the mystical meaning of: 'A virtuous woman (=the *Shekhinah*) is a crown to (=higher than) her husband' (=the 'Holy One, Blessed be He') (Prov. 12:4).

God's Sovereignty can also be referred to as His speech. Creation is brought about by the '*word* of the Lord'. This can be understood on the analogy of human speech. It is by means of speech that man gives expression to his thoughts and feelings, but it is also possible for man to conceal his true thoughts and feelings by saying the opposite of what he really thinks and feels. Speech is then used to conceal rather than reveal. In the same way, it is by means of the various combinations of letters[8] that God brings about the creative process. This is God's 'speech'.

But this is not always, as it were, a true expression of God's will, since evil, the 'Other Side', has also come into existence in the worlds in which God is revealed, and this, too, is for the greater fulfilment of God's purpose. Yet, since the final aim, God's ultimate will, is revealed only in the creative process by which the finite world comes into being, God's 'word', the expression of this fulfilment, is, in a sense, higher than all the other *Sephiroth*. Thus, it can be said that God conceals Himself in His speech, since so long as evil is unvanquished His purpose is unrealized. But this concealment will itself suffer concealment in the days of the Messiah, and then men will see only God. This is the mystical meaning of: 'I will hide, surely hide, my face in that day' (Deut. 31:18). This means that on 'that day', the day of the coming of the Messiah, God will 'hide' the 'hiding of His face' and He will be truly revealed, even in the world of 'speech'.[9]

The main purpose, then, of man's worship is to unite the Holy One, Blessed be He, with His *Shekhinah*. This means that in worship he learns to pierce the veil, so that he sees only God, so that God's simple unity is seen even in this finite world of division. It is the task of the worshipper to reflect deeply on the truth that the whole *Tzimtzum* process takes place only from our point of view. According to Aaron, the anthropomorphic term '*Adam Qadmon* ('Primordial Man', used of the Sephirotic realm in potentiality) gives expression to the idea that *Tzimtzum* can be understood, in some small measure, on the analogy of human intellectual endeavour. When a father, in his great love for his child, wishes to converse with the child, it is necessary for him to put himself into the child's mind, to adapt his thoughts to the child's limited mental capacity. The thoughts conveyed are those of an adult, but they are reduced in power so that the child may grasp them.

In similar fashion, God reduces His power by means of *Tzimtzum*, so that finite creatures may come into being.[10] But Aaron adds his usual rider that any analogy for the divine mysteries is bound to be inexact. The thought of the father as it is in itself and that thought as adapted to the needs of the child are two separate things, whereas, in reality, the thoughts of God, as it were, are the same before *Tzimtzum* as after *Tzimtzum*.[11] It is the powerful realization of this which constitutes worship.

The difficulty in worship is occasioned by the hindrances placed in the way of the realization of the truth that all is in God by the 'animal' or 'natural' soul. Aaron consequently embarks on a detailed exposition of the doctrine of the two souls.[12] The divine soul, the portion of the divine in man, mirrors the divine realm. Just as, from God's point of view, there is only simple unity, in which all separate powers and forces are included in their potentiality by virtue of the great marvel (*pele'*), so, too, in potentiality, the divine soul embraces in its simple unity all the separate and different human faculties.

The animal soul, on the other hand, mirrors the divine realm in its aspect of *Tzimtzum*, i.e. as it is seen from our point of view. Just as God in His process of revelation brings all the potential forces into operation and actualizes them in all their separateness, so, too, the animal soul infuses all the separate faculties of man, endowing them with vitality. It is thus in the nature of the divine soul to rise upwards to God, whereas it is in the nature of the animal soul to be separated from God. Hence there is constant tension in man's psychic life, the divine soul urging him upwards towards unification in God, the animal soul dragging him downwards to see only division and separateness. Out of this tension man can become spiritually creative. He can allow his divine soul so to bestir itself in quest of the divine unity that it comes to have an influence even on the animal soul. In this way, man's whole life is seen in terms of creative struggle. The turmoil in man's soul mirrors, in fact, the cosmic process in which the world of separation is ultimately connected with the world of unity. Moreover, since man's inner life does mirror the cosmic process, it can influence that process. Man's struggle for unity within his own soul, his search for that vision which sees only God, assists in the very process of uniting the Holy One, Blessed be He, with His *Shekhinah*.

On the basis of the Ḥabad doctrine, Aaron ingeniously explains a number of Scriptural verses where tradition records an alternative reading (*Qeri* and *Kethibh*). The oral version (*Qeri*) of Isaiah 63:9 is: 'In all their affliction He was afflicted' (reading *lo*, with a *waw*), but in the written version (*Kethibh*) the reading is: 'In all their affliction he was not afflicted' (reading *lo'*, with an *'aleph*). Similarly, in I Samuel 2:3 the oral version is: 'For the Lord is a God of knowledge, And by Him actions are weighed' (reading *lo*, with a *waw*). But in the written version the text reads: 'And by Him actions are not weighed' (reading *lo'*, with an *'aleph*). Finally in Psalm 100:3 the oral version is: 'It is He that hath made us, and we are His' (*lo*, with a *waw*). But the written text is: 'It is He that hath made us and not we (ourselves)' (reading *lo'*, with an *'aleph*).

Aaron's novel interpretation of all this is that the text as written refers to the point of view of God. From God's point of view, there is only simple unity. From that point of view, one cannot speak of God suffering in our afflictions or weighing our deeds or taking us to be His own. The oral version, on the other hand, refers to our point of view. From our point of view God is, indeed, involved in our sufferings; He weighs our deeds and we are His. It follows that, from man's point of view, worship is of the most tremendous significance in that it helps to produce these effects and causes God to reign in glory over His creatures. Man thus has a share in, even an effect on, the divine pathos as revealed to us. It is true that it is not legitimate to speak of this if we are thinking of God's point of view, (from this point of view it is, indeed, not legitimate to speak at all), but speak of it we must from our point of view, and here the consequences for action are highly significant, in that through man's worship there is an increase in the divine flow of grace.[13]

Following the conventional *Ḥabad* theory, with its roots in the *Kabbalah*, Aaron states that the true effect on the divine realm, from our point of view, can only be produced by Israel. Israelites alone have a divine soul and, unlike the Gentiles, their animal soul is derived from the 'Shell' (*Qelipah*) of *Nogah* ('Light') which is not entirely evil, but contains an admixture of good and evil. We have noted earlier that this is basically the standard *Habad* position, which Aaron, too, adopts. Therefore, the whole struggle for recognition of the divine, the conflict between the two souls with its effects on the cosmic process, takes place only in and through Israel's worship.

This is the basis of Aaron's mystical interpretation of: 'The Lord is high above all nations, and His glory above the heavens. Who is like unto the Lord our God, that dwelleth so high; that looketh down so low upon the heaven and the earth' (Ps. 113:4–6). As for the nations, it appears absurd to suggest that man's deeds can have any influence on the divine, since God is, for them, 'high' above all possibility of being influenced by events which take place in the finite world. From their own point of view they are, indeed, right in their contention, since they are incapable of seeing the divine, even here on earth. For them, all being is rightly divided into 'high' and 'low', into the realm of God and that of His creation.

But Israel perceives that God can 'look down so low', that from God's point of view there is neither 'high' nor 'low' and all is equally divine. The consequence is that Israel is able to see the eternal significance of man's deeds despite the fact, or rather because of it, that they take place in this finite physical universe. It is the task of man in his worship here on earth, using as he does the things of the material world, to remove all barriers between 'high' and 'low', so that God's glory may be revealed.[14]

The doctrine of the two souls is basic to Aaron's view, as it is to *Habad* thought in general. It is important to appreciate that Aaron does not depart from the standard Rabbinic view that the conflict within man is between the good inclination (*yetzer ha-tobh*) and the evil inclination (*yetzer ha-ra'*), and his freedom of choice depends upon which of these he follows. It might have been tempting for the *Habad* thinkers to identify the divine soul with the Rabbinic 'good inclination' and the animal soul with the 'evil inclination', but they were unable to do this for two reasons.

First, the animal soul contains both good and evil, unlike the 'evil inclination'. Secondly, the classical Kabbalistic view is that the divine soul, as a portion of *'En Soph*, is 'beyond good and evil' and can suffer neither improvement nor change. Aaron's view is, consequently, that God, in addition to giving man his two souls, endows him with freedom of choice by creating within him two warring spiritual forces (Aaron calls them 'angels'), one pulling him in the direction of the good, the other in the direction of evil. Both of these forces have their origin in man's animal soul. The function of the divine soul is to help man in his choice of the good. This is the deeper meaning, as Ḥabad sees it, of the old adage that God helps man to choose the good. It is the divine spark in man, his 'portion of God', which gives him the power to struggle against the evil in his nature. It is this which ensures, if only man wills it so, that the victory of the good inclination over the evil inclination is achieved. But, although it helps towards the outcome, the divine soul as a portion of God is not itself affected at all by the victory.[15]

The nature of man's worship is twofold. First, its aim is the rejection of evil in man's animal soul. This is achieved when man refrains from those things forbidden to him by God's will, i.e. when he keeps the negative precepts of the *Torah*, refraining from theft, deceit and the like. This is one way of achieving the higher aim of revealing the unity of God, even in the finite world of division. This is known as worship by 'coercion' (*'ithkaphya*), i.e. by allowing the good to encroach upon the realm of evil. But at this stage evil is subdued but not vanquished.

The second stage is the higher. It consists in turning darkness into light. The very evil in the animal soul is pressed into the service of the good. Man uses his bodily powers, infused with the vitality of his animal soul, to serve God in the performance of the positive precepts. The light of the divine unity is then revealed, even in the finite world. This aspect of worship is known as 'conversion' (*'ihaphkha*), i.e. the evil is turned to good through its elevation in the animal soul. Thus on the one hand, the evil in the animal soul is weakened by the starvation which results from denying its expression in forbidden acts and, on the other hand, it is elevated by being pressed into the service of the good in the carrying out of good deeds. This twofold process of worship is known as *birur* ('refinement'). The animal soul becomes progressively purged of its dross. The descent of the divine soul has no other purpose than this. As we have seen, the divine soul requires no perfection, being perfect in itself. It descends into the body in order to assist by its presence the refinement of the animal soul through the twin processes of 'coercion' and 'conversion'.[16]

There is a threefold division of all things into the good, the evil, the neutral. The precepts of the *Torah*, for instance, belong to the good. By carrying them out man increases the good and brings himself nearer to God. Things forbidden by the *Torah* belong to the realm of the evil and must be entirely rejected. Man must never attempt to use these as an aid to his pursuit of the good. In this sphere man's worship is only by the method of 'coercion' not 'conversion'. Man must not imagine that he can carry out evil acts in order to convert them into good through his good intentions. This, the method of 'conversion', applies only to neutral things, things in themselves neither good nor evil. These can be elevated if man uses them as an aid to the service of God, and by so doing he converts the evil in the animal soul into good.[17]

Aaron explains the technical Rabbinic term for the permitted —*muthar*—meaning 'untied', 'unbound', to mean that neutral things are in themselves free to be attached either to holiness or to impurity. If, for instance, man uses permitted food and drink as a means of gaining strength to serve God, or studies the physical sciences in order to gain a deeper knowledge of God's wisdom in creation, he makes the neutral serve the holy. If, on the other hand, he uses permitted food and drink as a means of self-indulgence or studies the physical sciences as an end in themselves, without associating their findings with the divine wisdom, then, in fact, he encourages the natural tendency of neutral things towards separateness and he thus makes them serve the 'Other Side', the aspect of impurity.[18]

The whole of man's worship is summarized in the verse: 'Depart from evil and do good' (Ps. 34:15). Man can 'do good' not only by carrying out the positive precepts of the *Torah* but by refining the neutral through the process of 'conversion'. But, with regard to those things forbidden by the *Torah*, man can worship God only by 'turning from evil', by rejecting them in totality. As examples of this Aaron quotes forbidden foods (pork and the like) and those sciences which are in direct opposition to the divine. These, he says, are the 'sciences of Egypt' (magic) and the anti-theistic philosophies. These can never be used in God's service, since they have their 'root' in the 'Other Side'. They enjoy existence only that man may reject them.

Aaron does not deny that it is sometimes possible for a great good to come from a great evil. Without sin, for instance, there could be no joy over the repentant sinner. But these matters belong to the mysterious ways of God, who may bring it about for purposes of His own. So far as man is concerned, he must never consciously embrace evil, even if his intention is to produce a greater good.[19]

A further example of the use of the neutral in the service of God is the way in which the *Torah* precepts rely on the material world. For instance, the parchment upon which phylacteries are written, the wool from which the 'Fringes' are manufactured, the citron used in worship on Tabernacles, all of these belong to the material world. In themselves they belong to the 'somethingness' of things (*yesh*) and are therefore in separateness from the divine. But when man uses them for the purpose of carrying out God's precepts, he elevates them and causes their 'somethingness' to become annihilated in the divine 'Nothingness'.[20]

Just as the power and might of a human king is seen to greater effect when he succeeds in imposing his rules even on distant isles and by the most intensive warfare, so, too, the whole purpose of the existence of evil is for God's glory to be revealed, even in its direct opposite.[21] Not that the illustration is exact. There cannot be, in reality, anything opposed to God. The existence of evil, the opposite of God's goodness, belongs to the great marvel (*pele'*) and is part of the greater mystery of how there can be a finite world at all. The illustration is intended only to convey this thought that a full and complete revelation must proceed from the contrary of that which is revealed. It is for this reason that man's rejection of sin is so significant. It is in this way that the very contrary to God is pressed into His service. This, too, is the mystery of the emergence of the loftiest souls from evil. Abraham was Terah's son, David was descended through Ruth from Moab, Akiba was a descendant of Sisera, and so forth. God's purpose is thus fulfilled in two ways. First, through Israel's worship the unification of God takes place. Secondly, God's glory is revealed in even greater measure when the good vanquishes the powers of evil.

This explains the otherwise puzzling statement in the Lurianic *Kabbalah* that the spiritual 'root' of Pharaoh was nourished from the 'back of *Kether*'. Pharaoh is the symbol of evil. How, then, can he be said to receive nourishment from *Kether*, the divine Will? But it belongs to the divine Will that the glory of God be revealed by contrasting it with its contrary. Nevertheless, it is from the *back* of *Kether* that the 'root' of Pharaoh is nourished, for the revelation of God's glory through its contrary does not belong to the normal channels of divine self-revelation. These are rather those of 'coercion' and 'conversion'. The revelation through contrast is important and belongs to the divine Will, but not in its most direct manifestation. This indirect purpose is called in the language of the *Kabbalah* the 'back' of *Kether*.[22]

We have seen that Aaron differs from his rival Dobh Baer on the question of ecstasy in worship. Both thinkers consider the attainment of ecstasy to be of the utmost importance, but Aaron is far more tolerant than Dobh Baer of ecstasy not entirely free from the taint of self-interest and self-awareness. Aaron is careful to point out that there is an ebb and flow in the life of worship. Man cannot always attain to ecstatic prayer. For all that, the aim of contemplation should be the attainment of ecstasy. At the very least, man should reflect on the idea that he is firmly resolved to become annihilated in God's unity. He therefore takes it upon himself immediately to turn from evil and do good, increasing thereby the sense of God's unity. This is far removed from true ecstasy in which the soul is lost in God, but, at least, there is firm resolve in the heart for such total annihilation to take place. In other words, the heart is involved even if it is not truly affected. But for man to dwell in contemplation without even this resolve is no more than an intellectual, academic exercise and does not merit the term 'contemplation' at all.

Aaron's illustration is taken from the life of a businessman. Such a man may come to see that a certain business deal he has in mind will be of great advantage to him. But it does not by any means follow that thorough contemplation that it is so will result in his determined and enthusiastic participation or that his enthusiasm will be evident all the time as he seeks to realize his aim. There will be times when his enthusiasm for the vision of success he has seen will carry him triumphantly along, but there will also be other times when it will all seem weary, heavy, burdensome. Nevertheless, he will persevere, because his heart tells him that his very livelihood depends on his carrying the deal to a successful conclusion. It is quite a different concept from a businessman idly contemplating a deal with which he is not personally concerned at all.[23]

We have noted that Aaron's interpretation of the unification of the Holy One, Blessed be He, with His *Shekhinah* is that man by his worship causes the distinction between God's point of view and ours to become exceedingly faint until eventually all is seen as God. There are two kinds of contemplation. The first is known as 'everlasting love' (*'ahabhath 'olam*). This is contemplation of the unity of God as revealed in the worlds, the unity as seen from our point of view. Here, man reflects on the tremendous mystery that there is a Power behind all things, by virtue of which they have come into being. This is known as the 'lower unification' and is also called 'external love', i.e. it is that love of God which derives from contemplation of His creation. It is this that is represented by the second (=additional) verse of the *Shemaʿ* ('Blessed be the name of His glorious kingdom for ever and ever').

The second kind of contemplation is represented by the first verse of the *Shemaʿ*. This is contemplation of God's unity as seen from His point of view, where all worlds are as naught before Him. This is called 'internal love', i.e. it stems from reflection on the inner spirit which infuses all things. This is less easy of attainment than 'everlasting love', but has deeper effects. It is therefore called 'abundant love' (*'ahabhah rabbah*). It is also known as the 'higher unification'.

Another set of symbols for these two types of unification is the following. Unification from the point of view of the worlds is the recognition of God as 'filling all worlds'. It is called God's *Shekhinah* and also His 'concealment', since the finite worlds are brought into being by means of God's 'concealment' in the *Tzimtzum* process. It is represented by the divine name *'Elohim*, the name for God's Power and Judgement. Unification from the point of view of God is a recognition of God as 'surrounding all worlds'. It is called 'the Holy One, Blessed be He' and is represented by the Tetragrammaton. The third verse of the *Shemaʿ* begins: 'And thou shalt love the Lord thy God...' because, as a result of the worshipper's deep reflection on these themes, he sees the underlying unity of all things and is moved to love God.

He perceives that in spite of the separateness of things as we see them there is, in reality, only the divine unity. He loves 'the Lord' (=the Tetragrammaton) 'thy God' (='*Elohim*), i.e. he sees that, in truth, there is no distinction between God's point of view and ours and that all is the blessed divine unity.[14]

Prayer is 'the time of battle'. This is to be understood in two ways. First, there is a battle during prayer. This consists of the severe and constant effort to distinguish between the sensation of ecstasy and self-awareness. The self must be brought into play in prayer so that it is moved in ecstasy. Unless this happens, all is cold and remote without true self-annihilation. There must be a self, with its sensations, for self-annihilation to happen. But self-sensation results in self-awareness. Here the task of the worshipper is to be deeply moved without sensing that it is *he* who is moved, without, as it were, the self calling attention to itself. The second type of battle is joined after prayer. The test of authenticity and ecstasy in prayer is whether the worshipper has been sufficiently moved to engage seriously in *Torah* study and the practice of the precepts as a result of his prayers.[25]

That stage of contemplation from the world to God (the stage of 'everlasting love') is represented by the prayers of the three Patriarchs. The stage of contemplation from God to the world ('abundant love') is represented by the prayer of Moses.

Aaron explains the two stages by means of a parable. A king had two sons. One stayed in the king's palace, the other was brought up in a distant village. The villager is obliged to learn gradually of the king's majesty, slowly emerging from the parochial and narrow to which he is accustomed, until he is able to enter the king's palace as a familiar. The son brought up in the king's palace has thought for nothing but the king's splendour, considering it to be his task even to go abroad to inform others of the great glory he has witnessed.

The Patriarchs recognized God by gradually raising themselves towards the divine. Moses saw the great King in His glory and endeavoured to spread the knowledge of this glory among creatures here below. Aaron implies that in miniature each worshipper can attain now to the stage of the Patriarchs now to the stage of Moses.

Another illustration of the difference can be given. A man may desire something because his mind tells him that it is good for him. When this happens, the intellect can be said to influence the will. But when the instinct of self-preservation is at work, when, for instance, a man is very hungry and longs for food, his intellect is influenced by his will and seeks to discover means for the will's gratification. So, too, man may attain to the desire for self-annihilation in God through reflection on the emergence of the worlds from the divine. This, the stage of the Patriarchs, is will resulting from contemplation. The stage of Moses is far more profound. It proceeds from the basic desire of the will for God and this will be fed by intellectual reflection.[26]

The true annihilation (*bittul*), whether of 'everlasting love' or of 'abundant love', was only realized by the Patriarchs and Moses. The Patriarchs alone attained to the full measure of 'everlasting love', Moses alone to the full measure of 'abundant love'. Yet, in miniature, each worshipper must strive to attain both these stages.[27] Aaron reverts to the warning that it is the greatest error to reject ecstasy. The truth is that, for the 'average men' (*benonim*), the war must be joined at all times, to struggle to attain the full sensation of ecstasy and yet to rise above self-awareness. 'The view of those lacking in knowledge who try to protect themselves against heart ecstasy, in love and fear with sensation, is mistaken. Their stupid argument is that where there is sensation there is a "something" which experiences the love. But they do not see how they imperil their soul by saying this. They keep their soul remote from the light of life and attach themselves to the materialistic mire of the animal soul, which descends to the lowest stage to become completely separated. Be desolate, O ye heavens for this!

'With respect to their bodily needs and worldly lusts they are attached with real sensation, and as a result of this powerful sensation they are entirely in a state of separateness and as remote from the light of God's blessed countenance as one can be. And yet when it comes to divine worship, which involves the annihilation of the self and its attachment to God, Blessed be He, they are suddenly afraid that they might experience a sensation of "somethingness" in ecstasy. Even if they do have this sensation there is, at least, some good in it. There is the category of annihilation, but mixed together with the aspect of "somethingness". But there is no good at all in the sensation of worldly things.'[28]

Aaron concludes the section of the work dealing with contemplation in prayer with a summary of his views on the stages of meditation. He writes:[29] 'This is the best advice for every soul in Israel which desires to serve God in this perfect worship. He should begin to worship by contemplating God's blessed unity, that all being in general and his own being, body and soul in particular, is annihilated in Him and included in His blessed unity by virtue of His marvellous power, as we have explained earlier.

'A great longing will follow on such contemplation to become attached in perfect love in His unity, to emerge from the confines of the limited and the separateness of "somethingness". As a result, he will attain to the stage of "abundant love", which stems from God's blessed essence, through appreciation in the mind that there is nothing apart from God and no being but His. He will then realize and appreciate the essence of his remoteness from God because of his very being, which is revealed in the category of "somethingness". He will then despise and denigrate this category of "somethingness" as it appears in him until, from his point of view, the body will not longer be seen as a separate entity. From this humility love will emerge with even greater power, so that he desires to ascend to his source with abundant love and tremendous longing.'

In Aaron's scheme, as we have already noticed, the practical precepts of Judaism are supremely important because these are the final expression of God's will. The basic principle here is, in language of the *Kabbalah*, that *Kether* (the divine Will) is 'higher' than *Ḥokhmah* (the divine Wisdom). Precisely because God is beyond all human comprehension, contemplation—in which the intellect is engaged—can never, in itself, bring man to God. The really vital link with the divine is provided by the practical observances of Judaism. The wearing of phylacteries and fringes and the other religious rites and ceremonies do not owe their value to any metaphysical symbolism, but to the opportunity they afford the worshipper of linking his life to God's will, which is identical with God Himself.

In Aaron's own words:[30] 'There is revealed specifically in all the letters of the Scroll of the Law, in their particular forms with their points and crowns, the actual will of God, Blessed be He. The Scroll becomes unfit for use if even one point is lacking. It is not enough that one understands the intention of the text. The letters represent the actual will of God in tangible form. For it is only by the actual deed that the power of *'En Soph*, Blessed be He, drawn down into it, can be awakened. As for wisdom and understanding, no thought can grasp Him at all.'

The particular difficulty, however, which Aaron finds here is the need for detailed observance each in its proper time and place. If the whole of the material world is the final revelation of God's will, how can certain acts in particular be the revelation of that will? Why, for instance, should special sanctity be attached to the objects used on the festivals? Why should wool fashioned in a special way as fringes be indicative of the will of God, rather than all wool which also owes its existence to God's will? On the deeper level, if all creation is God's will, how are the distinctions between the holy and the profane, the meritorious and unworthy, the permitted and the forbidden, to be justified? Does not the very suggestion that in certain acts God's will is revealed imply that in others it is not?[31] This is, of course, the old problem of reconciling the view that all is in God with the numerous legal distinctions made in traditional Judaism.

Aaron replies by means of an analogy.[32] The only way a man can give full expression to an idea he has is to expound it at length, using such devices as comparison and contrast. In the course of his detailed exposition, particularly if he has to suit it to minds inferior to his own, he is obliged to discuss many matters of only indirect relevance to the main theme. In fact, some of the matters he will be obliged to discuss will be in opposition to his central theme, but he will draw on them for the purpose of contrast, since an idea can only emerge with clarity when it is contrasted with its contrary.

Now, in a sense, it can be said that the whole exposition, including the irrelevant and contradictory notions, belongs to the central idea. In a sense, it all belongs to the full expression of the basic theme. But in another sense, it is clear that the basic idea is one thing, its detailed exposition another. The exposition is bound to contain some ideas very close to the central theme, others more remote and even contradictory to it. Similarly, God's will is revealed in the whole of creation. The whole of creation is a tremendous divine exposition of the original purpose that the light of '*En Soph* be revealed even in the 'somethingness' of things. But this exposition is bound to contain ideas very close to the original purpose, others more remote and others in direct opposition to it. Thus, forbidden things also belong to the divine exposition, but they serve as a contrast to the basic idea.

It is the will of God that these should enjoy existence, but only so that there should be a realm of the unholy to provide a contrast to the holy, in order to highlight the holy, as it were. Sacred things, on the other hand, belong to the original purpose in a far more intimate way. It is not nonsense to say that all things are, in a sense, the expression of the divine will and yet to go on to speak of that will as revealed, particularly in the precepts of the *Torah*. This is how Aaron, like many another Jewish mystic, defends the completely binding character of the *Torah* and rejects a mystical antinomianism.

It is true, says Aaron,[33] that, in addition to the contrast it provides to the holy, the forbidden can serve at times as a direct means to the holy. Elijah, for example, offered sacrifices, when this was forbidden, on a high place for the greater glory of God. Samson was led by God to take Delilah to be his wife. Although she was forbidden to him, David married Bath Sheba. The repentant sinner, say the Rabbis, is forgiven if he repents in love, to the extent that his sins are accounted as merits. But this use of evil as a throne for the good is rare and must never be consciously adopted. The evil and the forbidden exist only that the holy might be glorified through their rejection or destruction, except in those rare cases where God specially ordains that evil should serve the good directly, or where there is a special dispensation for this purpose, as in the case of Elijah. It is undoubtedly forbidden for man to sin in order that he might later elevate the evil into good by his repentance. This can only be achieved by the sinner who sinned because a 'spirit of folly' entered his heart and later gained the wisdom to repent.

With regard to man's daily, optional pursuits (i.e. those in themselves neither good nor evil), he can serve God by practising the annihilation of their 'somethingness'. When man eats and drinks to gain strength, for instance, or engages in business in order to have the means to serve God, he thereby elevates this whole world of the neutral and brings it to God. He removes from it the 'somethingness' and the separateness from God. He may, moreover, become aware, as a result of his concern for worldly matters, how remote he is in his human situation from the divine, and he may be moved to a spontaneous cry of anguish. This sincere cry from the heart at its remoteness from God is a powerful form of spontaneous worship.[34]

Very interesting is Aaron's interpretation of the Kabbalistic idea that the 'Written *Torah*' is represented by the 'Lesser Countenance' and the 'Oral *Torah*' by *Malkhuth*.[35] The Written *Torah* is God's wisdom in potentiality. It is that wisdom from God's point of view, before it has become actualized through the successive efforts of teachers throughout the generations. The actualization of this wisdom (this wisdom from our point of view) is the work of the great Rabbis and teachers of Israel, all of whom added something of their own towards the understanding and application of the *Torah*. When an idea is only in the mind in potentiality, its details are unknown even to the one who has it. By giving expression to his idea in teaching and exposition, he himself becomes more conscious of all its implications.

Or, to give a different illustration, a prince brought up in the king's palace knows instinctively how to behave in the presence of the king and has no need for the rules of protocol which are essential for the rustic who wishes to visit the palace. Thus, it is true that the details of how the *Torah* should express itself in human history is the work of the great teachers in each generation and, in so far as this is so, these are innovators. And yet all their innovations are implicit in the original Written *Torah*. In this way Written and Oral *Torah* can be seen as two sides of the same coin—the one God's wisdom in potentiality, the other as realized in human affairs. The one is the 'Lesser Countenance', God's wisdom from His point of view. The other is *Malkhuth*, God's wisdom from our point of view, His Sovereignty over His creatures. And the two are really one.

This explains the otherwise strange Rabbinic saying[36] that when Moses was escorted to the school of Akiba he was unable to understand Akiba's teachings, and his mind was set at rest only when he learned that all Akiba's teachings were 'given' to Moses on Sinai. For Moses knew the *Torah* at the stage of potentiality, while Akiba's task was to give it detailed application. Moses knew the *Torah* as it is from God's point of view.

Akiba knew it in the detailed manner in which it receives its expression from our point of view.

Aaron is much concerned with the question of the good motive. The standard Rabbinic view on this question is contained in the famous sayings of R. Judah in the name of Rabh that a man should always engage in *Torah* study and practice even if his motive is not for the sake of the *Torah*.[37] The motive for *Torah* engagement can either be 'for its own sake' (*lishmo*) or 'not for its own sake' (*shelo lishmah*). There are other Rabbinic sayings which frown on religious practice with an ulterior motive, and there is much discussion on the whole question in the classical sources. It is well known that the early *Ḥasidim* were severely critical of the learning and piety of their day on the ground that the motives of the scholars and pietists were frequently unworthy. True to his Hasidic background, Aaron understands Rabh's term 'not for its own sake' to mean where the highest motivation is lacking, where the deed is performed without any sincere intention at all. The highest motivation is for the sake of binding all the worlds to *'En Soph*. This is the meaning of 'for its own sake'. But where the motive is self-seeking and unworthy, e.g. to acquire fame or success or to feel superior to others the very practice of *Torah* becomes sinful.[38]

'Such a person draws down the divine to imprison it within a murky place of thick darkness and surrounds it with impenetrable walls. This can be compared to a king who commanded one of his subjects to bring him an object of great worth. Instead of bringing it to the king, he keeps it for himself, surrounding it with many walls so that the king cannot reach it. The will of God is automatically drawn down as a result of *Torah* practice, as we have stated, for no word or deed can fail to do its work of awakening God's essence, Blessed be He. It is not enough that he fails to become attached to and annihilated in God's will, but, on the contrary, he draws God's will to himself in the category of the "Shells". His punishment is therefore exceedingly severe.'

Just as the deed is the most significant thing of all with regard to the good, so it is with regard to evil. Merely for evil thoughts repentance is required, but when man gives concrete expression to evil in a deed, he provides a 'body' for the 'Shells'—the opposite of the divine—and only the most extreme form of penitence can suffice to regain the holy by shattering this 'body'.[39] Furthermore, just as there are the categories of 'greatness' and 'smallness' with regard to the holy (the stage of utter devotion and that of apathy), so it is with regard to evil. An occasional slip or lapse from virtue cannot be compared to determined plotting or planning of evil in which man allows himself to become involved with fervour and enthusiasm. The greater the vitality with which man sins, the more he imprisons the holy—the source of all vitality—within the net of the 'Other Side'.[40]

Thus, whatever deed a man performs, whether for good or for ill, he awakens thereby a divine force.[41] The difference is this that the good deed reflects ultimate truth, whereas the evil deed belongs in the 'false' category—from the ultimate point of view —of God's concealment. It follows that, while evil deeds can be revoked and reclaimed through repentance, the good deed is never lost, no matter what happens.

NOTES TO CHAPTER SEVEN

[1] *SA*, Introduction, beg., pp. 1a–13b. The text down to 'but all can benefit from parts of it at least' on p. 119 is based on this passage.

[2] The best edition of the *Qunteros Ha-Hithpa'aluth* is that of Warsaw, 1868, with a Commentary by Hillel of Parits, the whole under the title *Liqqute Bi'urim*. V. my translation, with an introduction and notes, under the title *Tract on Ecstasy*, Vallentine, Mitchell, London, 1963.

[3] V. the lengthy summary of his views by Aaron in *SA*, Introduction, *ibid.*, pp. 9a f., note beginning *u-bhazeh thabhin*. Here Aaron observes: 'You will understand from this how great is the error and lack of understanding of those who seek to reject heart ecstasy sensations. They argue that where there is heart sensation in worship the "somethingness" (*yesh*) is sensed. But the contrary is true. Where there is no heart sensation, the emotions of the animal soul remain in all their power to sense that "somethingness" which belongs to the evil side, so that the divine soul cannot be revealed at all, as in the above-mentioned illustration of the soil (and the silver). But when the heart is moved to ecstasy in the love of God, albeit that the "somethingness" is sensed in this love, then *da'ath* has the effect of creating a distinction, so that the sensation should stem from self-annihilation, from the desire to become one in God's unity, and it succeeds in removing that kind of sensation which stems from self.'

[4] V. *Tanya, op. cit.*, beg., Part I, Vilna, 1930.

[5] *SA*, *Sha'ar* I, Chap. 1, pp. 1a–b.

[6] *SA*, *ibid.*, Chap. 2, pp. 1b–3a.

[7] *SA*, *ibid.*, Chap. 3, pp. 3a–b.

[8] V. *Tanya*, Vilna, 1930, Part II, Chap., pp. 152–3.

[9] *SA*, *ibid.*, Chap. 5, pp. 4b–5b.

[10] *SA*, *ibid.*, Chap. 20, pp. 26b–27b.

[11] *SA*, *ibid.*, Chap. 21, p. 28a.

[12] *SA*, *ibid.*, Chap. 23, pp. 30b–32a.

[13] *SA*, *ibid.*, Chap. 25, pp. 34a–35b.

[14] *SA*, *ibid.*, Chap. 35, p. 49b.

[15] *SA*, *Sha'ar* II, Chap. 3, pp. 3b–4b.

[16] *SA*, *ibid.*, Chap. 4, pp. 4b–5b.

NOTES

[17] *SA, ibid.*, Chap. 5, pp. 5b–6b.

[18] *SA, ibid.*, Chap. 5, p. 6a.

[19] *SA, ibid.*, p. 6b; Chap. 8, p. 10a.

[20] *SA, ibid.*, Chap. 10, p. 12b.

[21] *SA, ibid.*, Chap. 16, pp. 19a–20b. The text to the end of this paragraph is based on this passage.

[22] *SA, ibid.*, p. 20b. *Cf. AH*, Part II, p. 34b.

[23] *SA, ibid.*, Chap. 34, pp. 50a–51a.

[24] *SA, Shaʿar* III, Chap. I, pp. 1a–3b.

[25] *SA, ibid.*, Chap. 2, pp. 3b–5a.

[26] *SA, ibid.*, Chap. 36, pp. 61a–62b.

[27] *SA, ibid.*, Chap. 39, pp. 68a–70a.

[28] *SA, ibid.*, Chap. 39, p. 68b.

[29] *SA, ibid.*, Chap. 39 end, p. 70a.

[30] *SA, Shaʿar* IV, Chap. 3, p. 5b

[31] *SA, ibid.*, Chap. 8, pp. 11a–b. *Cf. AH*, Part II, p. 3a.

[32] *SA, ibid.*, pp. 11b–13a.

[33] *SA, ibid.*, Chap. 10, pp. 15a–b.

[34] *SA, ibid.*, p. 16a.

[35] *SA, ibid.*, Chap. 15, pp. 23b–24b.

[36] *Men.* 29b.

[37] *Pes.* 50b.

[38] *SA, ibid.*, Chap. 34, pp. 52b–53a.

[39] *SA, Shaʿar* V, Chap. 1, pp. 1a–b.

[40] *SA, ibid.*, Chap. 2, pp. 2a–b.

[41] *SA, ibid.*, Chap. 4, pp. 5a–6b.

CHAPTER EIGHT

Rabbi Aaron's Scriptural Exegesis

We have noticed more than once in these pages the manner in which Aaron utilizes Scriptural passages of no apparent relevance to his theme for the purpose of conveying his own ideas. This should not be construed as a conscious reading into Scriptural verses of something the exegete knows perfectly well is not really to be found there. Aaron's principle here, like that of the earlier Kabbalists, is that, in addition to the plain meaning of a text, there is a higher meaning which is the true soul of the *Torah*. This higher meaning concerns the divine mysteries. The three Patriarchs, for instance, at the level of the plain meaning, are the three historical figures whose deeds are recounted in the book of Genesis. But on the level of the higher meaning they represent the three *Sephiroth—Ḥesed, Gebhurah, Tiphereth*.

From the historical point of view, to be sure, it is anachronistic to read Scripture as a series of Kabbalistic texts, but the Kabbalists themselves really seemed to have believed that the *Kabbalah* is revealed truth to which Scripture alludes, if only one learns to penetrate beyond the simple to the higher meaning. In a famous passage in the *Zohar*[1] we read: 'Said R. Simeon: "Alas for the man who regards the *Torah* as a book of mere tales and everyday matters! If that were so, we, even we, could compose a *torah* dealing with everyday affairs, and of even greater excellence. Nay, even the princes of the world possess books of greater worth which we could use as a model for composing some such *torah*. The *Torah*, however, contains in all its words supernal truths and sublime mysteries . . . Thus, had the *Torah* not clothed herself in garments of this world, the world could not endure it. The stories of the *Torah* are thus only her outer garments, and whoever looks upon that garment as being the *Torah* itself, woe to that man—such a one will have no portion in the next world. David thus said: 'Open Thou mine eyes, that I may behold wondrous things out of Thy Law' (Ps. 119:18), to wit, the things that are beneath the garment.

' "Observe this. The garments worn by a man are the most

visible part of him, and stupid people looking at the man do not seem to see more in him than the garments. But in truth, the pride of the garments is the body of the man, and the pride of the body is the soul. Similarly, the *Torah* has a body composed of the precepts of the *Torah*, called *guphe Torah* (='bodies', main principles of the *Torah*) and that body is enveloped in garments composed of worldly narrations. The stupid people see only the garment, the mere narrations; those who are somewhat wiser penetrate as far as the body. But the really wise, the servants of the most high King, those who stood on Mount Sinai, penetrate right through to the soul, the root principle of all, namely, to the real *Torah*." '

True to this conception, Aaron and the other Hasidic teachers[2] expounded, Sabbath by Sabbath and on the great feasts of the Jewish year, the weekly or festival portion of the *Torah* in such a way as to make the most unpromising material yield the metaphysical and psychological themes with which Hasidism is concerned. Most of the works of the early Hasidic masters consist of their weekly and festival sermons preached to their followers and later collected, generally by their disciples. Many of Aaron's expositions of this nature are to be found in his *Shaʿare Ha-Yiḥud We-Ha-'Emunah* and *Shaʿare ʿAbhodah*, but his *ʿAbhodath Ha-Levi* contains the record of his systematic preaching on the portions of the week from Genesis to Deuteronomy. The better to appreciate the method we shall quote here a number of Aaron's expositions.

In the book of Deuteronomy (2:11) we read of the giants, who dwell on the other side of the Jordan, called *ʿAnaqim* and *Rephaim*, and that the two are accounted as one. According to a Rabbinic interpretation (*Sot.* 34b), the *ʿAnaqim* were so called because, owing to their stature, 'they wore the sun as a necklace' (*maʿaniqim*). The word *Rephaim* Aaron connects with the root meaning 'to heal'. Aaron[3] sees these two types of giants as representing two gigantic spiritual attitudes, both at variance with the truth. The term 'sun' refers to the 'higher unification' (from God's point of view) in which all the multiplicity of creation is seen as embraced by the divine unity. It is as clear as the sun that, in reality, there is only the One. For man to reach this stage in contemplation is high enough. But there is an even higher stage at which man can see only the divine unity when it is more elevated than any thought of multiplicity whatsoever. The *'Anaqim* of the 'holy side' are those spiritual giants whose contemplative activity takes them so far aloft that the mind reaches 'beyond the sun'.

This type of contemplation produces a great longing in the heart for God. Since the mind has reached to a stage far higher than reason, it produces a love of God beyond all reason. The emotions awakened in this way are called *Rephaim*, because the purpose of all healing is to strengthen nature and, as a result of this deep love of God, man's natural emotions become united in his love for God. This is why Scripture states that the *'Anaqim* and the *Rephaim* are accounted as one. For that stage of contemplation represented by *'Anaqim* produces the stage of love represented by *Rephaim* and, conversely, because of man's powerful love, he can attain to the stage of contemplation that is higher than reason.

Now, whatever is present in the 'holy side' is also present in the sinister realm. In the realm of evil, too, there are the attitudes represented by *'Anaqim* and *Rephaim*. *'Anaqim* here represents that attitude which thinks of God as so elevated above all the worlds that He cannot be said to be in any way involved in the worlds. In the realm of the holy, the elevation of God above all worlds is for the purpose of the most perfect recognition of his complete unity. The separateness of things is transcended by the mind which reaches beyond all thought of separateness. But, in the realm of the sinister, God's elevation, far from encouraging self-annihilation, encourages separateness. As for the *Rephaim* stage, this means, in connection with the sinister, that man's emotions are given healing and strength, so that they can function adequately without God. The philosophy in which God is elevated beyond His creatures produces an attitude of emotional anarchy. The emotions are removed entirely from the dominion of the holy. Conversely, because man's emotions desire freedom from the restraints of the holy, they encourage him to believe in a philosophy of God's utter elevation above all worlds.

Og, King of Bashan, represents the most powerful of the gigantic demonic forces. 'For only Og king of Bashan remained of the remnant of the *Rephaim*' (Deut. 3:11). When the power of all the others is spent, Og's remains undiminished. Og is '*ugah*, 'the circle'. The circle is unbounded. Og represents the complete encirclement of man by his conviction that the worlds are separate from God. Imprisoned within the circle of his emotions, man senses only himself—the very opposite of the annihilation of selfhood in the divine. Such a man is entirely enclosed within the narrow confines of the 'somethingness' of things, even when his worldly lusts are dormant. It is not a case of failure to struggle against the unholy, but of drawing a magic circle to keep out the holy. Og is King of Bashan on the other side of the Jordan. Through Og the spiritual forces of the Holy Land remain in isolation, without the power to spread holiness to the world.

Og's iron bedstead was nine cubits in length (Deut. 3:11), for Og refuses to number *Kether* among the *Sephiroth*, so that the nine lower ones are detached from '*En Soph*. For Og the idea of the marvel (*pele'*) represented by *Kether* is not allowed to intrude. The Sephirotic world is detached from '*En Soph*, with the result that the lower worlds are left without the light of '*En Soph*. God's sovereignty is acknowledged, but His unity is denied. In the language of the *Kabbalah*, the *Sephirah* of *Malkhuth* is separated from its 'roots' in '*En Soph*.

The whole exposition here has many such brilliant applications of the Kabbalistic themes (as understood by Aaron) to the words of Scripture. Unreasonable though the whole method must seem to anyone with the slightest historical sense, it cannot be denied that, granted Aaron's premise that the mystical teachings constitute the authentic inner meaning of the *Torah*, he has succeeded in manipulating his texts with great skill.

The following is Aaron's interpretation[4] of: 'Thou shalt not see thy brother's ox or his sheep when they have strayed, and hide thyself from them; thou shalt surely bring them back unto thy brother' (Deut. 22:1). The term 'brother' represents the 'higher unification' in the 'World of Emanation'. There the *Sephiroth* are seen as completely united, with no divisions at all. The three *Sephiroth*, *Ḥesed*, *Gebhurah* and *Tiphereth*, at that stage, represent respectively the higher love, the higher fear and the higher compassion (*Tiphereth* is also known as *Raḥamim*, 'Compassion'). In man's psychic life these three correspond to man's completely disinterested love, fear and compassion, in which there is no selfhood at all, only annihilation in the divine.

But in the 'lower unification', as the *Sephiroth* are revealed in the Worlds of Creation, Formation and Action, *Ḥesed*, *Gebhurah* and *Raḥamin* appear as separate. It is man's task to learn to see them as united in marvellous unity even from this point of view. This, too, is applied to man's psychic life. There is, indeed, no change whatsoever with regard to the first of the three *Sephiroth*, *Ḥesed*. Man's love for God is the same whether it stems from the higher unification or the lower. But with regard to *Gebhurah* and *Raḥamim*, there is much difference between their manifestation in the higher and lower unification. Since, in the lower unification, these are seen in their separateness, it is all too easy for them to become detached from the divine unity. *Gebhurah* then becomes either the fire of worldly desires or the sensation of the self in worship. The worshipper loves and fears God, but is conscious that he does so, and there is selfhood in his worship. His compassion is similarly filled with self. His is an attitude of self-pity. He is sorry for himself (not for God's sake) that he is remote from God. The term 'ox' represents the fierce power of *Gebhurah*, the term 'sheep' the mildness of *Raḥamim*. Hence the mystical meaning of our verse is: Even in the lower unification man should not see *Gebhurah* (=the 'ox') and *Raḥamim* (=the 'sheep') as if they had gone astray from their complete unification in '*En Soph* (=the aspect of 'thy brother'). For if this happens he will, in fact, be hiding himself from them; their true purpose will be overlooked and selfhood will gain the upper hand. He must surely bring them to the category of 'brotherhood' in which all multiplicity is overcome, and there is complete unity in the divine.

In Deuteronomy we read: 'Justice, justice shalt thou pursue' (Deut. 16:20), a plain enough verse as it stands. But for Aaron, the chief interest in his expositions is to uncover the mystical meaning of Scripture. Hence he refers, in his comment on this verse,[5] to the term 'justice' as representing *Malkhuth*. This is the revelation of God's sovereignty which apportions each thing in the material world to its allotted place. It is the principle by which justice is done to every detail in God's creation, by means of which God's will is revealed in the world of multiplicity and separateness. *Malkhuth* is the lowest of the *Sephiroth*. But its 'root' reaches back to the will of God and, from this point of view,

Malkhuth, the final expression of God's will, is highest of all. There are thus two aspects of *Malkhuth*. There is the lower 'Justice' (=*Malkhuth*), by means of which God's will is expressed in the world of multiplicity, and there is the higher 'Justice', in which the source of all this is in God's inscrutable essence, where there is only simple unity. The task of the worshipper is to proceed from his recognition of God's unity, amid all the multiplicity of the material world, to the acknowledgement that from God's point of view all divisions are embraced by His complete unity. Hence from 'Justice' (=the 'lower Justice'), one must ascend in contemplation (='pursue') to 'Justice' (=the 'higher Justice').

It is instructive to see how Aaron and his master, Schneor Zalman, treat, in their different ways, the passage containing the law of the first-born: 'If a man have two wives, the one beloved, and the other hated, and they have borne him children, both the beloved and the hated; and if the first-born son be hers that was hated; then it shall be, in the day that he causeth his sons to inherit that which he hath, that he may not make the son of the beloved the first-born before the son of the hated, who is the first-born' (Deut. 21:15–16).

Naturally, neither Aaron nor Schneor Zalman overlook the plain meaning of the text. This belongs to what the *Zohar*, in the passage quoted above, calls 'the body of the *Torah*'. For these teachers, the law of the first-born is the revealed will of God in this particular concrete human situation. But the mystical meaning is for them the deeper meaning of the text, though they differ as to what the mystical meaning is. It is highly probable (in view of the different mystical meanings of a given text found, in this type of literature, even in the writings of the same author) that the two teachers would not have considered their different interpretations to be mutually exclusive. Just as a verse has a plain and a mystical meaning, it can have more than one mystical meaning.

Schneor Zalman[6] sees the 'two wives' of the verse as the two souls, the divine and the animal. The divine soul is man's beloved wife, the animal soul his hated wife. The two rivals compete with one another, particularly at the time of prayer, when the divine soul longs for the nearness of God while the animal soul tugs at man with thoughts of self. But when a man has to fight for the things he loves, his affection for them is increased by the struggle.

Similarly, when the divine soul in man competes with his animal soul, thereby purifying it of the evil and selfhood it contains, the resulting love for the divine is far more powerful than it could have been if there had been no struggle. This is the meaning of the verse in which it is stated that the first-born son is of the hated wife. The sons born to the soul are the emotions of love and fear. Therefore, if man emerges victorious from the struggle between the divine and animal soul (the 'beloved wife' and the 'hated wife'), the first-born 'child' is that of the 'hated wife', the love and fear of God which stem from the struggle with the evil within are greater than they could otherwise have been without the animal soul's opposition. When the animal soul, too, is coerced into loving God, the love and fear of God are all the more powerful.

In Aaron's interpretation,[7] the 'man' of the verse is 'the Holy One, Blessed be He' (=the *Sephirah*, *Tiphereth*) and the 'two wives' are two aspects of the *Shekhinah* (=*Malkhuth*). In Kabbalistic symbolism, Jacob, the third Patriarch, represents *Tiphereth*, and Rachael and Leah, his two wives, the two aspects of the *Shekhinah*.[8] In Aaron's interpretation of the Lurianic symbolism, Leah represents that aspect of the *Shekhinah* in which it turns towards the 'world of concealment', whereas Rachael represents that aspect in which the divine is revealed in the lower worlds of multiplicity and separateness, the worlds of 'somethingness'.

Since the whole purpose of creation is for the worlds of 'somethingness' to become annihilated in God's unity, the divine purpose receives its ultimate fulfilment through Rachael. This is why Rachael is more loved than Leah. Furthermore, man can be said to love an idea he can grasp and fully understand, but to hate an idea he must accept on trust without the capacity of understanding it. The Rachael aspect of contemplation is intelligible. Man reflects on such things as the spiritual insignificance of a mere physical act in relation to the spoken word, and of the spoken word in relation to the mind. In this way he comes to appreciate that all separateness in the world is as nothing before God. This type of contemplation (from the world to God) is near at hand for man. Because he can understand it, he can be said to love it. But contemplation on the Leah aspect (from God to the world), that God is beyond all human comprehension and that all worlds come into being by His unfathomable will, this concerns a concept utterly beyond man's intellectual grasp. He cannot love it, even though he accepts it on faith. However, the most powerful emotions of love and fear stem from the Leah rather than from the Rachel type of contemplation. Precisely because man reflects on the 'otherness' of God, he is moved to worship in wonder. This is why the 'first-born' is of the 'hated wife'. In other words, meditation on the 'world of concealment' is emotionally more rewarding then meditation on the 'world of revelation', but this is because the former is less comprehensible. The sense of utter wonder here is greater. But, for all that, it is in the 'world of revelation' that God's highest, because ultimate, purpose is fulfilled.

One of the clearest statements of Aaron's views is found in his exposition[9] of the story of Balaam and his ass (Num. 22:2–35). Here Aaron writes: 'It is well-known that the ultimate purpose of creation is that God's will to reign should be revealed, and there can be no king without subjects. In this is God's perfection revealed. For it is revealed that there is none else and no other apart from Him, and this revelation is made particularly in the category of "else" and "other", so that it should be the same after the world was created as it was before the world was created.

'The purpose is that all the inhabitants of the world should recognize God's wonders. For the finite emerged from the *'En Soph*, the Limitless, detached and simple to the ultimate degree of simplicity. There emerged worlds without number, numerous *Tzimtzumim* (plural of *Tzimtzum*), an infinite number of details among creatures, each creature different from others in size, appearance and temperament. How can these have emerged from the *'En Soph*, Blessed be He, than Whom there is none else, and to whom can He be revealed? Even the notion of a "will" cannot be applied to Him, Blessed be He. For the notion of willing applies only to man, confined by Time and Space. Of such a being it can be said that in the past he did not will and later changed his mind to will something he lacked apart from himself.

'None of this is, God forfend, in any way applicable to God,

Blessed be He—a time when He does not will and a time when He does. Does He lack anything, God forfend? This is, indeed, His perfection. For if you say that the '*En Soph*, Blessed be He, cannot be in the finite then you place limits on His perfection by suggesting, God forfend, that His power is confined to the Infinite and does not extend to the finite. A perfect sage, for instance, is not truly perfect unless he has the capacity of limiting himself so as to be able to converse even with the most inferior. But, in reality, the analogy is inexact. For with regard to the sage, who concentrates on the mind inferior to his own and thus limits his wisdom, the wisdom required for communication is something other than his own great wisdom, and the inferior mind is also other than the mind it causes to suffer change.

'It is otherwise with regard to the blessed, limitless light of '*En Soph*. For He suffers no change, God forfend, even after He has concentrated Himself ($=Tzimtzum$) into His creatures. He, Blessed be He, is exactly the same in the upper and lower worlds. The worlds and concealments do not hide or conceal Him, Blessed be He, in any way; but the concealment and hiddenness are themselves the power of His essence, since there is nothing apart from Him. How this can be, it is beyond the power of any creature to grasp.

'All this is, however, as it is in reality, from God's point of view, Blessed be He. But, from our point of view, there is a force which proceeds from Him, Blessed be He, by means of which He does not appear as He really is, but is hidden and concealed, so that to us there is revealed real "somethingness" and separateness. But since this is so, then it would seem, God forfend, as if His perfection and true Being are not revealed in the "somethingness" of things. Consequently, His perfection is revealed through Israel, the people near to Him, who are called "the limbs of the King". This can be understood by analogy. Man's soul is only revealed through his limbs—in the hand's power to act, the eye's power to see, and so on. It follows that it is through the bodily organs that the true perfection of the soul becomes revealed, to animate the body in every particular. Similarly, this is what happens through the souls of Israel, the people near to Him, through their worship in reciting the *Shema‘* and prayer, in which there is united in one Being the

Tetragrammaton and *'Elohim*. In this way, all the details seen by our eyes (because of the effects of the name *'Elohim*, which limits and conceals the light of *'En Soph*, Blessed be He, so that they appear, from our point of view, as "somethingness" and as really separate) are united to the uttermost limits in one Being so that there is nothing apart from Him and nothing separate from Him.

'For "the souls of Israel ascended in thought", that is to say, their "root" is higher than thought (i.e. ascended *above* thought), for they are called "the people near to him" (i.e. to His essence, *above* His thought). It is because of this that they possess the capacity for sacrificing their all, even in concealment, and for converting all their desires and will to God and His will, Blessed be He. In this way God's unity, Blessed be He, is revealed, that in heaven above and on earth beneath there is, in reality, none else, after the creation of the world, exactly as before the creation of the world.'

This is why, continues Aaron, Balak wished Balaam to curse Israel, because they both desired that the 'somethingness' of things should be seen in detachment from God. For them the 'somethingness' of things is the final purpose of creation, an aim in itself, not a means to an end. Their philosophy was that life was to be enjoyed for its own sake and that this was the will of God. To them nothing was forbidden, because, in their view, God had created this world of 'somethingness' and separation with all that is in it, for man to enjoy. Israel is the great enemy of this idea. For Israel, the people near to God, whose divine soul is a portion of God Himself, the 'somethingness' of things exists only for its ultimate annihilation in God.

The Hebrew word *'athon*, used for 'ass' in the narrative, is formed of the letters *'aleph, taw*, final *nun*. The letters *'aleph* and *taw* are the first and last letters of the alphabet. According to the *Kabbalah*, it is by means of the letters of the Hebrew alphabet that God created the world, i.e. the letters represent those spiritual entities involved in divine creation. The long final *nun* represents the drawing down of the divine creative activity into the finite world. It is this which enables the finite world to endure. But whereas Israel seeks always to keep the letters attached to their source, to draw the world back into God, Balaam smites the *'athon,* i.e. he seeks to detach the world of 'somethingness' from its roots in the divine. This is why Balak says to Balaam: 'Behold there is a people come out of Egypt; behold they cover the face of the earth, and they abide over against me' (Num. 22:5).

Israel abides over against Balak in that Israel's desire is for the annihilation of the 'somethingness' of things in the divine. This people Israel has come out of Egypt (=*Mitzraim*, from a root meaning 'to confine', 'to restrict'). They seek always to rise above all confinement and limitation of the divine. And they cover the face of the earth, i.e. they allow the divine to conceal the 'somethingness' of things. For Balak and Balaam the earth covers the divine. Israel brings God down into His creation so that the divine covers the earth.

From the above examples it will be seen that Aaron is true to his Hasidic background in his exegetical method. Like other Hasidic teachers, including his master, he seems to have believed that there is scope for originality in exegesis, even though, as we have seen, he is careful to deny that there can be any really original thought in *Kabbalah*. The distinction appears to be this, that the actual truths of the *Kabbalah* cannot be arrived at by the exercise of the human reasoning powers, but must be received by tradition. These are divine truths for the Kabbalists, and can only be revealed by God Himself. Here the human mind can only elaborate and expound. But since these are divine truths and the *Torah* is divine, there is scope for the human mind to discover where the Kabbalistic ideas are recorded in the *Torah*.

NOTES TO CHAPTER EIGHT

[1] III, p. 152a.

[2] *V. AH*, Part II, pp. 11a f., where there is a lengthy exposition on Lev. 23:15 f. which Aaron's editors claim is copied from Aaron's autograph notes made after he had heard a sermon by Schneor Zalman. *Cf*, for a similar exposition, *AH*, Part III, Deut., pp. 8b f.

[3] *AH*, Part III, Deut., pp. 1a–2b.

[4] *AH*, Part III, Deut., pp. 18b–19b.

[5] *AH*, Part III, Deut., p. 12b.

[6] *Liqqute Torah*, Deut., Vilna, 1878, pp. 75–76.

[7] *AH*, Part III, Deut., pp. 16b–18b.

[8] *V.* Gershom G. Scholem: 'On the Kabbalah and Its Symbolism', translated by Ralph Manheim, Routledge and Kegan Paul, London, 1965, pp. 149 f.

[9] *AH*, Part II, pp. 55a–56b.

CHAPTER NINE

Summary

Aaron's system cannot easily be summarized. Dealing as it does with all the intricate detail of the Lurianic *Kabbalah*, of which it is an interpretation, its strength and a good deal of its significance depend on a close familiarity with the Lurianic system. For all that, it is possible to sketch the main principles as they appear in Aaron's works.

The key to the whole system is Aaron's particular solution of how *deus absconditus* can become *deus revelatus*. Aaron's answer is to draw a distinction between God's point of view and our point of view. To the question of how the finite world, with its error, evil, imperfections and multiplicity, can have emerged from the Infinite, the perfectly good and true, the *Zohar* replies by means of the *Ten Sephiroth*. The Lurianic *Kabbalah* replies that God withdrew from Himself into Himself (*Tzimtzum*) in order to leave room for the world.

Aaron, following Schneor Zalman but with important elaborations, accepts both these theories as part of the same description of the divine creative process, but expounds the whole matter in an entirely fresh and original way. On the earlier theories in their plain meaning there are two aspects of Deity. God in His aspect of *'En Soph* is completely unknown. God in His revelatory aspect brings the finite world into being by means of *Tzimtzum* and the *Sephiroth*, because He desires to reign over His creatures, because it is in the nature of the good to have recipients for its bounty. But the difficulty here is to avoid dualism. There are not two Gods, one unknown, the other revealed, but only one. Yet if this is so, how can God be both unknown (and unknowable) and revealed? To this Aaron gives the very radical reply that, indeed, the whole revelatory process is only real from our point of view, not from God's. From God's point of view there is no will to create, no *Tzimtzum*, no Sephirotic realms, no world and no creatures. The whole revelatory process is only as seen by us—by the human beings who are themselves part of that process. The distinction is no longer between two aspects of Deity, but between two ways of looking at Deity.

However, when it is said that the whole revelatory process, including the very idea of revelation, and its culmination in the multiplicity of the finite world, has no reality from God's point of view, some qualification is necessary. The world and its creatures, *Tzimtzum* and the *Sephiroth*, are not an illusion fostered by God, not a cosmic conjuring trick. It is not so much that these have no reality at all from God's point of view, but that they are transcended by the greater Reality that is God's unity.

The illustration of the sun's rays is given by both Schneor Zalman and Aaron in trying to convey the meaning of this very difficult concept. A ray of light is real enough, though it is produced by the partial screening of the light itself. For Aaron, the ray is present even in the light itself, but there it is included in the light's unity. God is omnipresent, so that the 'rays' (=the revelatory process) are, from His point of view, always included in His unity. The divine concealment does its work of screening, as it were, the divine light, so that the rays can be seen in their separateness and multiplicity. Since the very screening is an essential part of the whole process, this, too, is embraced by God's unity. Modern investigations into the meaning of religious language certainly pose a problem here for the whole of Aaron's system. Aaron himself, in seeking to describe how God can be both present and not present, how we can have our point of view at all if it is not God's point of view, invokes the idea of the marvel or wonder. The matter, he says, is too deep for human understanding. From the human point of view, Aaron admits, there is a contradiction involved in the whole conception, but the laws of human logic do not apply to God's thought, which is, indeed, not thought at all as we know it, but 'higher' than thought. But the serious objection here is that the only language we have is human language and in that language to say that $A = $not-$A$ is to talk nonsense; it is to fail to make any significant statement at all. God can perform wonders, but it is logically meaningless to say that He can in marvellous fashion make A equal not-A.

In any event, Aaron is prepared to accept the marvel that there are these two points of view, God's and our own. This leads to the significance of man's worship. Man's task in worship is to rise above the distinction and see only the divine unity. This aim is achieved in two complementary ways. The first is by means of intense meditation on the theme that all is in God and that there is 'none else'. Contemplation can either proceed from the world to God—the 'lower unification'—or from God to the world—the 'higher unification'. In the 'lower unification' the mind proceeds gradually from reflection on the divine vitality by which the grossest manifestation of matter endures to the divine vitality in higher forms. It proceeds from stones to animals to humans to angels, from the soul to the higher worlds and from these to the *Sephiroth* and to *'En Soph*. In this type of meditation the whole process is brought back into God.

In the 'higher unification' the process is reversed, the mind descending from meditation on the inscrutability of *'En Soph* down through the whole chain of being as infused with the light of *'En Soph*. The aim of both types of meditation is for the worshipper to see, beyond all screens and concealment, that there is only the perfect unity of God. Contemplation is not an academic exercise. The heart must respond and will respond, if there is authenticity in the contemplation. The worshipper 'senses' God's presence. The test of authenticity in contemplation is whether the heart responds in rapture.

But important though contemplation is it cannot, in itself, help man to rise upwards to *'En Soph*. In contemplation only the intellect and the emotions are involved, and *'En Soph* is utterly beyond thought and feeling. The second way, therefore, for the worshipper to attain to a realization that all is in God is that of carrying out the practical observances of Judaism—the giving of charity, the avoidance of evil acts, the performance of the rituals. In all these, man becomes involved in the material world. The practical observances afford man the opportunity of obedience to God's will in the realm (the material) that is most remote from Him.

Since God's ultimate purpose is that the most remote should be drawn into His unity, these observances link man with God's will and, since in God will and essence are one, this means that the worshipper is linked with God Himself. Contemplation is essential, for without it the mere deed is lifeless, a mere mechanical act. But it is in the deed that the vitality achieved through contemplation must be given expression.

To man alone is given this tremendous role of bringing about the unification, because man is created in God's image and he mirrors the whole creative process. He is of earth, yet his soul reaches to heaven. Man is himself the symbol of the divine unity, and he alone, therefore, can achieve it. Like his Creator, man acts and he has will, thought and feeling. Moreover, in addition to his 'animal soul' (the life force which animates him), he has a 'divine soul'. This latter is an actual 'portion of God', a part of *'En Soph*, as it were, in deepest concealment.

Man's true self, therefore, is divine, which means that, paradoxically, man does not truly find 'himself' in selfhood, but in 'annihilation' in the divine. The more man is self-conscious in his worship, the greater the influence of the 'animal soul', the further he is from his true self. The divine unity cannot be met where there is selfhood. Where this is present, man becomes separated from God, and the whole unification process, which depends on him, is frustrated. Conversely, when man allows his divine soul to elevate him to become annihilated in the divine, he discovers his true self. He is then a unity and sees only the divine unity in all creation. In this way, he achieves the unification he was created to achieve, and the whole of creation is, as it were, absorbed back into God. The tension between selfhood and annihilation in the divine can never be completely resolved in this life. There is constant conflict between the two. The whole of man's life is a quest for unity.

Man, in this context, means Israel. Aaron does not deny that non-Jews can acknowledge God as Creator and worship Him. But in Aaron's system (and in *Ḥabad* generally), Israel alone has the gift of the divine soul and Israel alone, therefore, is capable of achieving the perfect unification. Implying as it does a qualitative distinction between the souls of Jews and non-Jews, this aspect of Aaron's teaching will commend itself to few modern minds, quite apart from the extremely radical doctrine itself that God Himself is in man. Certainly the *unio mystica*, in this sense, is very unconventional in Jewish thought.

No one can study a system such as Aaron's without becoming aware of the striking parallels it affords with Far Eastern religious thought. Aaron's views are, of course, monotheistic, not monistic.[1] The unity to be sought, for Aaron, is the unity of God. And he is completely traditional in his attitude towards the Law. Aaron is a loyal devotee of *Torah* and the precepts. He is activist in his religion; contemplation is only the means of infusing observance with vitality, whereas observance is an aim in itself, the supreme form of divine worship.

For all that, one cannot help comparing Aaron's 'somethingness' of things in all their divisions 'from our point of view' and the true unity from God's point of view, with the Vedānta philosophy of *māyā* ('illusion', 'appearance'), the multiplicity of the universe, produced by *avidyā* ('ignorance'), when in reality there is only One, the *brahman-ātman*. In the Upanishads, however, *māyā* means 'cosmic illusion', a concept which, as we have seen, Aaron rejects.[2] There is not much difference, moreover, between Aaron's 'divine soul' as a portion of *'En Soph* and the famous Sanskrit *tat tvam asi* ('That art thou'), that the *ātman*, the eternal self, is one with *brahman*, the absolute principle of all being.

There is no need to postulate any kind of direct influence of Far Eastern thought on the *Kabbalah*, though this is certainly possible. The mystical quest quite naturally tends to express itself in the same terms, despite differences in cultural background. In any event, there can be no question of either Aaron or any of the other *Ḥabad* thinkers having any knowledge of Far Eastern thought.

Nor are the parallels limited to Far Eastern thought. Ideas such as Aaron's are found among Christian and Muslim mystics. His doctrine of negation is Eckhart's: 'God is without name, for no one can say or understand anything of Him ... Hence if I say: "God is good", this is not true. I am good, but God is not good ... If I say further: "God is wise", this is not true, I am wiser than He. If I say also: "God is a being", this is not true; He is a being above being and a superessential negation.' Aaron's multiplicity of things embraced by the divine unity is Eckhart's: 'If we say that all things are in God, we understand by this that, just as he is without any distinction in his nature, and yet absolutely distinct from all things, thus also all things are in him in the greatest distinction and yet not distinct, and first of all because man is God in God: in the same way, then, as God is not distinct from the lion and yet is altogether distinct from it, so also, in God, man is not distinct from the lion and is yet absolutely distinct from it. Thus it is also with the other things.'[3] And Aaron's teaching that man can come to see only God is paralleled in the Persian ode of the dervish, Baba Kuhi of Shiraz:

> 'In the market, in the cloister, only God I saw:
> In the valley, on the mountain, only God I saw.
> I opened mine eyes and by the light of His Face around me,
> In all the eye discovered, only God I saw.
> Like a candle I was melting in His Fire:
> Amidst the flames outflashing only God I saw . . .
> I passed away into nothingness, I vanished,
> And lo, I was the All-living—only God I saw.'[4]

It is only in Jewish thought that Aaron's views are unusual.

Aaron's significance in the history of Jewish thought is that he is both the most systematic and the most consistent representative of the *Ḥabad* philosophy, as well as being the one thinker of this school who does not shrink from drawing the most radical conclusions from its premisses. In his work there is found a highly unconventional acosmic or panentheistic philosophy. For Aaron, monotheism is not only the doctrine that there is only one God or that God is unique but that, beneath the multiplicity of the finite world, there *is* only God and that all things are embraced by His perfect unity. Aaron's passion, to which he dedicated his life, was to achieve the 'lower' and the 'higher' unification. More than any other traditional Jewish thinker, he is the great seeker of God's unity.

NOTES TO CHAPTER NINE

[1] *V.* Chap. VIII: 'Monism *Versus* Theism', and Chap. IX: 'Theism *Versus* Monism' in *Mysticism Sacred and Profane,* by R. C. Zaehner, Clarendon Press, Oxford, 1957, pp. 152–97.

[2] *V.* Hasting's *Encyclopedia of Religion and Ethics,* article Māyā, Vol. 8, pp. 503–5.

[3] The two passages from Eckhart's Sermons are quoted in *Master Eckhart* (Men of Wisdom Series), by Jeanne Ancelet-Hustache, London, Longmans, 1957, pp. 55 and 56. *Cf.* David Baumgardt: *Great Western Mystics,* Columbia University Press, New York, 1961, who refers to the parallels between Ḥabad and Eckhart.

[4] R. A. Nicholson: *The Mystics of Islam,* London, 1914, p. 59, quoted by Sidney Spencer; *Mysticism in World Religion,* Pelican Books, 1963, p. 320.

APPENDIX

A Letter of Rabbi Yitzhak Isaac Epstein of Homel

Reference has been made earlier to Rabbi Yitzhak Isaac Ha-Levi Epstein of Homel (1780–1857), disciple of Schneor Zalman and Dobh Baer. In the controversy between Aaron and Dobh Baer he favoured the latter. Yitzhak Isaac's collected writings were published posthumously in four volumes under the title *Ḥanah 'Ariel* (Berditchev, 1912). At the end of the volume containing his essays on the Sabbath and other topics there is also a letter (pp. 4b–5a of the final section), the authenticity of which there is no reason to doubt.

The letter bears no date, but was written some time after the death of Schneor Zalman and is in the nature of a defence of Dobh Baer's teachings against the charge of heresy which had been directed against them. There is no record of the identity of the addressee, but Bunim ('*Mishneh Ḥabad*', *op. cit.*) is of the opinion that it was addressed either to Aaron himself or to one of his followers. The letter is somewhat difficult to decipher completely, but is worth quoting in full for the light it throws on the themes dealt with in this book. The translation from the Hebrew is mine and is fairly literal.

Yitzhak Isaac is fond of breaking into Yiddish when he wishes to express his views with greater precision. It seemed best to leave the Yiddish in transliteration, but I have placed the English translation of the Yiddish expressions in square brackets. Short explanations of the more difficult passages, as well as other information, have also been included in square brackets. The passage in round brackets is Yitzhak Isaac's.

It was the frequent habit of the *Ḥabad* writers to leave sentences unfinished, ending these with the Hebrew equivalent of 'etc.', and this procedure has naturally been followed in the translation. I have divided the letter into paragraphs to make for easier reading, even though these do not occur in the original.

Rabbi Yitzhak Isaac's Letter

'I am writing this after having found rest from my anger and solace for the pain caused by the many words, etc. which had as their purpose the denigration of our group as people of iniquity, with our lord, master and teacher [Dobh Baer] at our head, etc. As I recall former days when we loved one another with a deep love, how can I help at least speaking to you in serenity and tranquility?

'Listen, please, my beloved friend! *Nit zog has ve-shalom az dos is apikorsus u-philosophia.* [Do not say that this is, God forfend, heresy and philosophy.] *Rak zog dos is* [Rather say that it is] true belief by virtue of which the dead are revived, so that the dry bones *zollen margish zein* [should experience] the living God. *Un alle Ḥasidim* [And all Ḥasidim], especially the disciples of our lord, master and teacher [Schneor Zalman] his soul is in Eden, *hoben die emunah* [have this belief]. *Un sie vert dehört al pi rov in Shemonah ʿEsreh.* [And it is generally sensed when reciting the Eighteen Benedictions.] That is to say, after all the goodly meditations while reciting the Songs of Praise and reading the *Shemaʿ*, with the higher and lower unification [*v. supra* p. 154], *vert noch dem dehört* [there is then sensed that], in Yiddish, *altz is Gott* [all is God]. *Un ḥosekh de-qelipoth Nogah shteht fun veiten un hört vie die velt is a velt un ess shat gor nit un is gor nit mevalvel die emunah.* [And the darkness of the Shell of *Nogah* stands from afar and senses that the world is a world and this does no harm and in no way confuses the belief.]

(This is different from the reading of the *Shemaʿ* where the world is not sensed in the effort involved in contemplation. This is because contemplation is on the theme of how it is before Him. For it is well-known that the reading of the *Shemaʿ* involves the unification of Father and Mother but Prayer involves the unification of the Lesser Countenance and the Female [*v. supra* p. 53]. The Prayer is an exposition of the *Shemaʿ* that it might be explained even for us etc. And I do not come here to expound etc.)

'On the contrary, the darkness of the Shell of *Nogah* [*v.*

supra p. 123] derives nourishment from this to do evil to him and to confuse him for ever and swallow him up. [i.e. far from there being any contradiction between sensing the world and recognizing that all is God, the selfhood involved in sensing the world is only possible because this, too, is from God and offers a temptation for man to be drawn into separateness and extreme self-awareness.] And it works in two ways. [I.e. the correct way to resolve the tension between the recognition that all is God and the pull of selfhood.] Either he becomes exceedingly abhorrent in his own eyes at being so remote from the clearly perceived truth, or he takes pleasure in warming himself at the light from afar, to convert the evil waters, etc.

'All Ḥasidim share this belief. As for the *Mithnaggedim* [the opponents of the Ḥasidim], even those who are not, etc., they do not have this belief, except in exceedingly great concealment, exactly as it was when Israel was in Egypt. *Hagam Gott is bei sei auch altz zu globen auf Ihm im kol zeh hoben sei kein ort nit le-emunah zu az altz is Gott.* [Even though for them, too, all is possible with God, they have, none the less, no room for this belief that all is God.] *Ober Ḥasidim hoben dos le-olam.* [But Ḥasidim always have this belief.] *Un ganz alte Ḥasidim* [And the very old Ḥasidim], the disciples of our teacher Rabbi Menahem Nahum of Tchernobil [d. 1789], his soul is in Eden, *hot dos bokea gevehn gor vild* [broke out in extremely wild fashion in entertaining this belief] because they did not engage sufficiently in contemplation. But among the disciples of our lord, master and teacher [Schneor Zalman]. his soul is in Eden, the belief was expressed with greater subtlety and in two ways.

'The first is as above. The second way is that when thought reaches *auf Ihm alein az hu be-tziur ophan* [to God Himself, it is applied as follows]. *Es is mehr nito vie Ehr alein un vider kehren altz is Gott.* [There is nothing but God alone and once again all is God.] This is the true method of the ebb and flow of the soul and her source in the upper worlds, reaching and yet not reaching to the light of *'En Soph*, extending to all infinity.

'But this belief is in the category of "smallness". It can be compared to a baby who clearly recognizes its father. The infant's recognition is exactly the same as the adult. The adult son has no greater recognition that this is his father than has the baby. But the child has no knowledge at all of how the father is his, for the child belongs neither in the category of knowledge nor in that of the need for knowledge. The adult, on the other hand, knows well that it is his father. He understands perfectly how a son comes from the very essence of his father. But the adult can only know the reason that he is his father's son, if he has the child's knowledge that this man is his father. But if he lacks the child's recognition that this particular person is his father, his reason can in no way tell him that he has come from this person's very essence. It follows that the knowledge the adult possesses is based only on childlike recognition and is not founded on reason in itself, etc.

'So it is with regard to our subject. The adult stage of this belief, explained in the "Tract on Contemplation" [by Dobh Baer, *v. supra* p. 25], has no room for and no connection with human reasoning. It belongs rather to faith, in the category of pure faith, upon which the adult perception is based. This latter consists of a strengthening of the powers of the divine soul, that she might know her faith with sound reason. However, it does not belong at all in the category of comprehension, but in the category of faith, which is the power of the soul, etc. There is no need to spend more time on this for, as the above-mentioned tract states, even in the category of descent and clothing in the garments of comprehension, the act of comprehension can only extend to the category of 'Adam Qadmon [*v. supra* p. 51]. But it does not extend even to the beginning of the "line" [*v. supra* p. 51], for even the thought of 'Adam Qadmon cannot grasp this, as we have said.

'This adult form of perception stems from two things. It can be compared to very fine intricate engravings on a brilliant surface. One who looks superficially at this surface will not see that there are designs there at all. One who peers more intently will see that there is something on the surface, but will not be able to discover what it is until he has availed himself of a good eye lotion, prepared by a skilled healer, to strengthen his eyesight. Now, in reality, this illustration should have been sufficient for the understanding of the matter to which it is applied. But nowadays it is a time of trouble, and someone may take it to mean that there are designs of the kind mentioned "there". Consequently, it is necessary to state that the purpose of the illustration is to convey two ideas.

'The first is that one must stop to look. The second is that one must avail oneself of the good lotion of a skilful healer. This is provided by the goodly, precious Hasidic expositions which we heard from the mouth of our Lord, master and teacher [Schneor Zalman], his soul is in Eden, These offered healing to the divine soul only, to increase her powers that she might find goodly reason in her belief. And the benefit was not derived from the mere sweetness of his exposition of the words of the *Torah*, but was by virtue of the light which shone in his holy words. This strengthened the power of the soul to recognize with goodly flavour the matter of the aforementioned belief *as altz is Gott* [that all is God], even *die velt* [the world] sensed at the time in darkness in particular, as above. *Un mehr nisht as Ehr alein* [And that there nothing but God Himself] in the category of ebb and flow as above.

'And I, the writer, *hob maki gevehn* [did spew out] my mother's milk over this belief. For in the above-mentioned category of "smallness" our lord, master and teacher [Schneor Zalman], his soul is in Eden, planted it into me in his *Torah* exposition of the verse: "Shall bake your bread in one oven" [Lev. 26:26, this seems to be the meaning of this rather cryptic sentence]. And the belief began to flower and grow through the efforts of his son our lord, teacher and master [Dobh Baer], the Rabbi, long may he live! But my eyes were weak, so that I was unable to perceive it properly, and I wanted to hear it explained verbally. For this purpose I wrote many petitions and made many requests and entreaties, but our lord, master and teacher [Dobh Baer] rejected me time and again. I was sorely distressed and tortured, until it came about at last that my petition was successful, and he immediately promised to tell me Hasidic doctrine in private audience. Afterwards, it so happened that ten people were present there, including Rabbi Yitzhak Hayyim of Darvayo. What need is there for me to say much about the *Torah* he expounded at that time! In brief, I remained in a state of trembling, not knowing whether it was day or night. After he had finished speaking, there shot through me like an arrow the light, power and strength of the afore-mentioned belief to the extent that there awakened in me at that time a desire to shout it aloud in the streets, until something came into my mind to persuade me that I should not do so. I do not recall a hint of what this reason was, but a firm resolve has remained in my heart from that time onwards. As God and my soul live, there is not a single word of exaggeration in this.'

Reading between the lines of this letter, we can see that Yitzhak Isaac is concerned to defend Dobh Baer's reliance on human reasoning in describing the mystery that all is God. We have noted earlier (*v. supra* p. 85) that Dobh Baer had been attacked on these grounds, and it seems that this was precisely one of Aaron's complaints against Dobh Baer's system. Yitzhak Isaac retorts that it is simply untrue to say that Dobh Baer relies on human reasoning for the *attainment* of the belief that all is God. This can hardly be true, in any event, since the belief itself is held by all *Ḥasidim*. It is only the *Mithnaggedim* who have no room for this belief or, at the most, only have it in 'great concealment', i.e. without being at all aware of it. What, then, is the role of reason? The function of reason is to add savour to the belief. Without the reasoned exposition of it, provided by Dobh Baer, the belief is immature. It is like the instinctive awareness of an infant that the man he recognizes is his father, without being able to understand what a father means. The contents of this letter throw further light on Aaron's demands (*v. supra* p. 83) that the use of human reasoning in this matter must be severely controlled by the observance of the conditions he regards as essential.

Index

Aaron, 40
Aaron of Starosselje,
  birth, 12
  discipleship, 12
  children, 13
  followers, 14
  discourses, 14, 16
  letters, 16
  relationship to teachers and colleagues, 23–24, 84–86
  exegetical method, 140–51
Aaron b. Zewi of Opatow, 57
'Abba ('Father'), 36, 53, 160
'Abhodath Ha-Levi, 14, 16, 19, 140f.
Abraham, 31, 39, 127
Abraham the 'Angel', 65
Abraham of Kalisk, 74
acosmism, 11, 15, 73, 157
'Adam 'Illaya, 41
'Adam Qadmon, 41, 48, 51–52, 121, 162
Agus, J. B., 46
Akiba, 127, 135–6
Altmann, A., 89
annihilation, 66, 67, 118, 127, 134, 146, 149
annihilation of self, 20, 68, 70–71, 79, 81, 93, 97, 115f., 130, 131, 143, 144, 155, 161
anthropomorphism, 41, 98
approbation, 17, 19–21
'Arikh, 53–54, 119
Aristotle, 46
Ashkenazi, B., 49
'ayin, 66–67
Azriel of Gerona, 45

Baba Kuhi of Shiraz, 157
Balaam, 147, 149, 150
Balak, 149–50
Bath Sheba, 134
Baumgardt, D., 75, 158
benoni, 118, 131
Berditchev, 23
Berkeley, 75
Besht, 24, 56, 57, 58, 70, 80, 82
Binah, 32, 34, 36–38, 41–43, 64, 93, 115
breaking of vessels, 52, 54–55
Broydé, I., 62
Buber, M., 75

Bunim, H. I., 74, 75, 111, 112, 159

Cairo, 49
chain of being, 43, 154
Chesterton, G. K., 88
Chashniki, 20, 21
Christianity, 47, 156
Coercion and conversion, 125f.
contemplation, 13, 20, 24, 58, 65, 67, 70, 71, 79, 87, 113–37, 138, 154–5, 157, 160–4
controversy between A. and Dobh Baer, 12–14, 25, 85–86, 115–17, 128, 159–64
controversies between *Tzaddiqim*, 60
Cordovero, 32, 37, 44, 45, 46, 49, 77, 94
Creator and creation, 27f., 49–52, 68–69, 96, 100–1, 147
Cremona, 49

Da'ath, 64, 114
David, 40, 127, 134, 140
debhequth, 59, 78
deism, 11, 68
Delilah, 134
Demiurge, 27, 46
demythologize, 28
deus absconditus, 29, 94, 152
deus revelatus, 94, 152
Dobh Baer of Lübavitch, 12, 14, 21, 23–25, 74, 75, 85–86, 89, 115f., 128, 159–64
dualism, 27, 98, 152
Dubnow, S., 23, 26, 62, 63, 75

Eckhart, 156, 158
ecstasy, 12–13, 86, 115, 128, 130, 131
Edom, 52
Eleazar b. Pedath, 17
Eleazar b. R. Simeon, 31
Elijah, 18, 29, 51, 77, 82, 134
emanation, 27, 33, 50, 96, 134
'En Soph, 27–63, 66, 68, 72, 90–112, 124, 133, 134, 136, 143, 144, 147–8, 149, 152, 154, 155, 156
Ergas, J., 55
Esau, 39
evil, 52, 54–55, 58–59, 121, 125f., 137, 142f.

165

INDEX

Ezekiel, 67, 82

Far Eastern thought, 65, 155, 156
Flew, A., 112
Four Worlds, 43, 51–52, 80, 97, 109, 143–4
freewill and God's foreknowledge, 103–5, 112

Gadiyoch, 24
Gaon of Vilna, 45, 51, 62
Garden of Eden, 29, 70
Gebhurah, 38–39, 40–43, 91, 140, 143–4
Gikatilia, 45
Ginzberg, L., 44, 48
Glenn, M. G., 89
Gnosticism, 27, 41, 46
Godhead, 28

Ḥabad, 12, 13, 14, 15, 16, 19, 21, 22, 23, 24, 25, 50, 51, 56, 57, 58, 61, 62, 64–76, 77, 80, 88, 93, 96, 113, 115, 116, 118, 119, 123, 124, 125, 155, 156, 157, 158, 159f.
Habermann, A. M., 74
Hartshorne, C., 23
Hasidism, 13, 15, 16, 25, 48, 50, 51, 57, 60, 63, 64, 65, 71, 85, 86, 136, 141, 150, 160, 161, 164
Hayyim Raphael of Starosselje, 13
Hegel, 23
Ḥesed, 38–39, 40, 41–43, 91, 140, 143–4
Hezekiah, R., 47
Hielmann, H. M., 23–25, 74
Hillel b. Meir of Parits, 14, 74, 138
Hillmann, D. Z., 74
Hod, 39–40, 41–43
Ḥokhmah, 30, 31, 32, 33, 34, 35, 36–38, 41–43, 64, 93, 115, 132
Holy Spirit, 18
Homel, 14
Horodezky, S. A., 23, 44, 62
Hume, 75
humility, 70, 132
Husik, I., 112

Ibn Ezra, 102, 112
illusion, cosmic, 96, 100, 153, 156
Imitatio Dei, 59
'*Imma* ('Mother'), 36, 53, 160
Infinite and finite, 27, 50, 52, 60, 66, 83–84, 91f., 96, 97, 107, 148
Isaac, 39

Isaac the Blind, 45
Isaac of Homel, 14, 111, 159–64
Isaac b. Sheshet, 47
Isaac of Vitebsk, 19
Isaiah, 82
Isaiah Horowitz, 12
Ishmael, 39
Islam, 53, 156, 158
Israelite, 31

Jacob, 39, 146
Jacob b. Idi, 17
Jacobson of Shklov, 14
Jethro, 105, 106
Jerusalem, 49
Jews, 68, 98, 123, 155
Johanan, R., 17
Joseph, 40
Judah, R., 136
Judah Laib, brother of S.Z., 24

Kabbalah and Kabbalists, 12, 18–19, 22, 27f., 40, 41, 44, 45, 46, 47, 49–63, 64, 67, 72, 73, 77–85, 90, 91, 94, 96, 102, 104, 119, 149, 150, 156
Kalisch, I., 44
Kant, 66, 75
Kether, 30, 31, 32, 33–37, 64, 66, 93, 94, 119, 127–8, 132, 143
Koretz, 26, 62
Krause, K. C. F., 23

Landau, E., 47
Leah, 146–7
Lemberg, 16, 19, 25
Levites, 31
Liady, 23, 25
'line' (*qaw*), 51, 55, 162
Liqqute 'Amarim, 15
logic and God, 102, 153
love and fear of God, 79, 129f., 142, 144, 146
Lübavitch, 13, 14, 22, 69
Luria, Isaac, 22, 43, 45, 49–63, 82, 119, 127, 146, 152

Macquarrie, J., 23
Maggid of Meseritch, 24, 56, 62, 64, 65, 66, 70, 80, 82
microcosm, 41
Maimonides, 28, 103, 104
Maimon, Solomon, 23

INDEX

Malkhuth, 31, 32, 38, 40–43, 93, 97, 119, 120, 135, 143, 144–5, 146
Mantua, 49
Maor ʿEnayim, 26
'marvel' (*peleʾ*), 18, 68–69, 95, 96, 99, 100, 103, 104, 109–10, 119, 120, 122, 127, 143, 153
mashal, 83–86
Meir Ibn Gabbai, 45
Menahem Mendel of Lübavitch, 13, 14, 21, 69
Menahem Nahum of Polotsk, 20
Menahem Nahum of Tchernobil, 26, 161
Messiah, 52, 53, 82, 109, 121
Michael David, A.'s son, 14, 21
Miskolc, 16
Mithnaggedim, 161, 164
mitzwoth, 87, 125, 127, 130, 132, 154
Mohilev, 12
monism, 156, 158
monotheism, 27, 28, 155, 157
Mordecai Francis, 49
Moses, 40, 63, 77, 93, 106, 107, 108, 111, 130, 131, 135
mythology, 28
mystery, 101
mysticism, 71, 79, 88, 124, 134, 156

Naaman, 105, 106, 107
Nahman of Bratzlav, 59–60
Nathanson, J. S., 19, 21
nature, 72–73
Neo-Platonism, 29, 45, 46
Netzaḥ, 39–40, 41–43
New Year, 69
Nicholson, R. A., 158
Nogah, 67–68, 160
Nothing, 31
Nuqwah ('Female'), 54, 120, 160

Og King of Bashan, 142–3
ʾOr Ha-Meir, 26
originality, 18–19
ʾor maqiph, 72
ʾor mithlabhesh, 72
Orsha, 12, 23

panentheism, 11, 15, 23, 157
pantheism, 11
Parits, 14
partzuphim, 53f., 89
pegam, 53

Pharaoh, 127–8
Philo, 41
Phinehas of Shklov, 24
Plato, 41
Polotsk, 20, 21
prayer, 97, 108, 109, 115, 117, 128, 130, 132, 148, 160
priest, 31

Qelipoth, 47, 54, 67, 68, 123, 136
Qeri and *Kethibh*, 123
Qunteros Ha-Hithbonanuth ('Tract on Contemplation'), 25, 89, 162
Qunteros Ha-Hithpaʿaluth ('Tract on Ecstasy'), 25, 75, 115f., 138

Rabh, 136
Rachael, 146–7
Rahab, 105, 107, 108
Raḥamim, 143–4
Ratner, I. S., 44
reason, 18
Reese, W. L., 23
Reshimu, 51
Ricchi, I. H., 55
Rodkinsohn, M. L., 74
Roth, Leon, 23
Rubin, S., 45, 47
Ruth, 127

Safed, 49
St. Petersburg, 23
Samson, 134
Sanskrit, 156
Sarah, 31
Schneerson, F., 23
Schneor Zalman of Liady, 12, 14f., 19, 20, 21, 22, 23, 24, 25, 64–76, 80, 81, 84–85, 86, 87, 101, 103, 111, 115, 116, 118, 145, 151, 152, 153, 159–64
Scholem, G. S., 23, 44, 45, 46, 62, 151
'Seer' of Lublin, 85
Sepher Yetzirah, 44
Sephiroth, 22, 27–63, 84, 91f., 94, 95, 97, 99–101, 104, 140, 143, 144, 152, 153, 154
Sephiroth, diagram of, 42
sexual imagery, 28, 40–41
Shaʿare ʿAbhodah, 15
Shaʿare Ha-Yiḥud We-Ha-ʾEmunah, 15
Shaʿar Ha-Tephillah, 16
Shabbethai Zewi, 53

167

INDEX

Shekhinah, 40, 47, 53, 77, 79, 119, 120, 121, 123, 129
Shklov, 14, 15, 20, 21, 24
Shemaʿ, 69, 79, 129, 148, 160
Simeon, R., 30, 31, 34, 140
Sisera, 127
Sitra ʾAḥara, 54, 126, 137
Slavita, 15, 26
Slonim, 14, 25
snail, 58, 63
Sod Qedoshim, 16
soul, 67–68, 84, 91, 95, 113–14, 122f., 138, 146, 155
Space, 50, 51, 56, 72, 73, 147
Spencer, S., 158
Spinoza, 23
Starosselje, 12
Steinmann, E., 23, 74

Talmud, 83, 87, 102
Tanya, 15–16, 68, 75, 76, 86, 87, 89, 116, 118, 138
Tchernobil, 26
Teitelbaum, M., 23, 44, 62, 74, 75, 76, 112
Terah, 127
Tetragrammaton, 41–42, 56, 58, 72, 93, 107, 119, 120, 129–30, 149
Theism, 11, 27, 158
Time, 41, 50, 60, 72, 73, 147
Tiphereth, 38–39, 41, 42, 140, 143, 146
Tiqqun, 52, 53, 54
Tiqqune Zohar, 29
Tishbi, I., 44, 45, 46, 47, 62
Torah, 87, 97, 108, 109, 125, 130, 134, 135, 136, 140, 143, 145, 150, 156, 163, 164
Torah, soul of, 141
Trinity, 47
Tzaddiqim, 60, 118
Tzawaath Ha-Ribhash, 59, 63

Tzimtzum, 22, 49–63, 64, 65, 84, 91, 96, 97, 98, 99–101, 103, 105, 106, 107, 108, 109, 120, 121, 122, 129, 147–8, 152, 153

unification, 20, 40, 54, 77, 79, 93, 97, 99, 100–1, 119, 120, 121, 123, 127, 129, 144, 145, 154, 155, 157
unio mystica, 11, 155
Upanishads, 156

Vedanta, 156
via negativa, 28f., 94f.
Vilna, 15
Vital, Hayyim, 45, 49, 62, 67, 75, 82
Vitebsk, 14, 19, 21, 25

Waite, A. E., 44
Walden, A., 23
Warsaw, 16, 19
Weiss, J. G., 48
Weiwow, L., 23
White Russia, 14
worship, 87, 113–39

yesh, 66, 67, 68, 70, 106, 115, 118, 127, 131
Yesod, 39–40
Yiddish, 159
Yitzhak Hayyim of Darvayo, 164

Zaehner, R. C., 158
Zeʿer ('Lesser Countenance'), 53–54, 119, 120, 135, 160
Zeev Wolf of Zhitomer, 26
Zeitlin, H., 75
Zewi Hirsch of Chashniki, 20–21
Zewi Hirsch of Zhydatchov, 85, 89
Zohar, 27–63, 89, 90, 94, 108, 119, 140, 145, 152
Zolkiew, 63